THE HIDDEN PLACES OF

NORTHUMBERLAND AND DURHAM

Including Northumberland, County Durham,
Tyne and Wear and the Tees Valley

By Peter Long

Published by: Travel Publishing Ltd, Airport Business Centre,
10 Thornbury Road, Estover, Plymouth, Devon PL6 7PP

ISBN13 9781904434771

© Travel Publishing Ltd

First published 1992, second edition 1995,
third edition 1998, fourth edition 2001,
fifth edition 2003, sixth edition 2005,
seventh edition 2008

Printing by: Latimer Trend, Plymouth

Maps by: ©MAPS IN MINUTES/Collins Bartholomew (2008)

Editor: Peter Long

Cover Design: Lines and Words, Aldermaston

Cover Photograph: Heatherslaw Corn Mill,
Cornhill-on-Tweed, Northumberland

Text Photographs © www.picturesofbritain.co.uk
and © Bob Brooks, Weston super Mare
www.britainhistoricsites.co.uk

All advertisements in this publication have been accepted in
good faith by Travel Publishing and have not necessarily
been endorsed by the company.

All information is included in good faith
and is believed to be correct at the time of going to press.
No responsibility...

This book is sold subject to the condition that it shall not, by
way of trade or otherwise, be lent, resold, hired out or
otherwise circulated without the publisher's prior consent in
any form of binding or cover other than that in which it is
published and without a similar condition including this
condition being imposed on the subsequent purchase.

Foreword

This is the 7th edition of the *Hidden Places of Northumberland & Durham*. The guide has been been fully updated and in this respect we would like to thank the Tourist Information Centres in Northumbria for helping us update the editorial content. The guide is packed with information on the many interesting places to visit in the area. In addition, you will find details of places of interest and advertisers of places to stay, eat and drink included under each village, town or city, which are cross referenced to more detailed information contained in a separate, easy-to-use section to the rear of the book. This section is also available as a free supplement from the local Tourist Information Offices.

Northumberland offers the visitor plenty of picturesque places to visit such as the Kielder Forest, the Cheviot Hills, Holy Island, and the many miles of attractive coastline. Hadrian's Roman Wall also stretches across this largely unspoilt county. *County Durham* is blessed with an incredibly strong history that runs deep with industrial heritage. The landscape still shows evidence of coal mining traditions, but the spoil heaps and pit heads have now all but disappeared. The county encompasses the beautiful and historic City of Durham and, like its northern neighbour, has an impressive number of castles, churches and historic houses.

The Hidden Places of Northumberland & Durham contains a wealth of interesting information on the history, the countryside, the towns and villages and the more established places of interest. But it also promotes the more secluded and little known visitor attractions and places to stay, eat and drink many of which are easy to miss unless you know exactly where you are going.

We include hotels, bed & breakfasts, restaurants, pubs, bars, teashops and cafes as well as historic houses, museums, gardens and many other attractions throughout Northumbria, all of which are comprehensively indexed. Many places are accompanied by an attractive photograph and are easily located by using the map at the beginning of each chapter. We do not award merit marks or rankings but concentrate on describing the more interesting, unusual or unique features of each place with the aim of making the reader's stay in the local area an enjoyable and stimulating experience.

Whether you are travelling around Northumberland & Durham on business or for pleasure we do hope that you enjoy reading and using this book. We are always interested in what readers think of places covered (or not covered) in our guides so please do not hesitate to use the reader reaction form provided to give us your considered comments. We also welcome any general comments which will help us improve the guides themselves. Finally if you are planning to visit any other corner of the British Isles we would like to refer you to the list of other *Hidden Places* titles to be found to the rear of the book and to the Travel Publishing website.

Travel Publishing

Did you know that you can also search our website for details of thousands of places to see, stay, eat or drink throughout Britain and Ireland? Our site has become increasingly popular and now receives over **500,000** visits annually. Try it!

website: www.travelpublishing.co.uk

Location Map

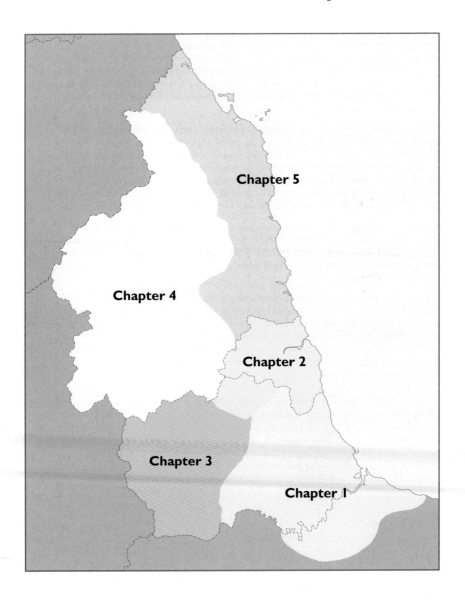

Contents

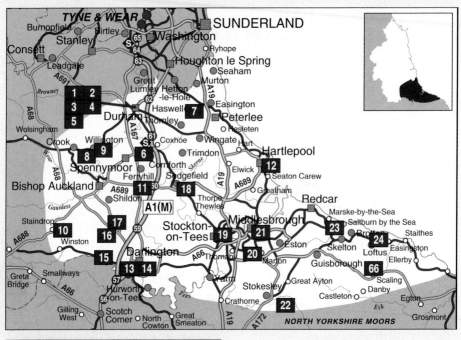

South & Central County Durham and the Tees Valley

County Durham's prosperity was founded on coal mining, and nowhere is this more apparent than in the central and southern parts of the county. Coal has been mined here for centuries, but it wasn't until the 18th century that the industry was established on a commercial basis. When the railways arrived in the early 19th century, the industry prospered, creating great wealth for the landowners, and frequently great danger and misery for the miners. Now that the industry has all but disappeared, the scars it created are being swept away. Spoil heaps have been cleared or grassed over, pitheads demolished and old industrial sites tidied up. Colliery villages such as Pity Me, Shiney Row, Bearpark, Sunniside and Quebec still exist – tight-knit communities that retain an old-style sense of belonging and sharing, and even in the most unprepossessing of villages there are delightful surprises to be discovered, such as the near-perfect Saxon church at Escomb.

Coal may have been king, but County Durham's countryside has always supported an important farming industry, and Central and South Durham still retain a gentle landscape of fields, woodland, streams and narrow country lanes. This area stretches from the East Coast to the Pennines in the west, and from the old border with Yorkshire in the south to the edge of the Tyne and the Wear conurbations in the north. Within this area there are picturesque villages, cottages, grand houses, museums, snug pubs, old churches and castles aplenty.

The coastline too has been cleaned up. An 11-mile coastal footpath snakes through the district of Easington from Seaham Hall Beach in the north to Crimdon Park in the south. Much of it is along clifftops with spectacular views down onto the beaches. This coastal area has recently been designated as a National Nature Reserve. Parts of what were County Durham, Cleveland and North Yorkshire have been incorporated into an area now known as Tees Valley, which includes the towns of Darlington, Stockton-on-Tees, Hartlepool, Middlesbrough and Saltburn-by-the-Sea and is blessed with many reminders of a rich maritime heritage. Captain Cook was born in Middlesbrough in 1728, and his story is told in the Captain Cook Birthplace Museum in that town. In nearby Stockton is a replica of his ship HM Bark Endeavour. At Hartlepool lies HMS Trincomalee, the oldest warship afloat. Saltburn's coast is a recognised part of the 36 miles of Heritage Coast, and Redcar is home to the oldest lifeboat in the world, housed in the Zetland Lifeboat Museum.

Travelling around the region the visitor is also constantly reminded of its rich social, industrial and Christian heritage. The Romans marched along Dere Street in County Durham, and in the 9th and 10th centuries holy men carried the body of St Cuthbert with them as they sought a place of refuge from the marauding Vikings. The railways were born in the county in 1825, with the opening of the famous Stockton and Darlington Railway.

Dominating the whole area is the city of Durham - one of Europe's finest small cities. It was here, in 1832, that England's third great university was established. The towns of Darlington, Stockton-on-Tees, Hartlepool and Bishop Auckland are all worthy of exploration.

Durham Cathedral and River Wear

1 LA SPAGHETTATA

Durham

A friendly, popular Italian restaurant close to the Castle.

see page 90

2 66 CLAYPATH

Durham City

An ideal base for exploring the North East with comfortable rooms and a hearty breakfast prepared fresh to order.

see page 90

DURHAM CITY

'A perfect little city' with 'the best cathedral on Planet Earth' – the words of travel writer Bill Bryson in his book *Notes from a Small Island*.

Arriving in Durham by train, the visitor is presented with what must be one of the most breathtaking urban views in Europe. Towering over the tumbling roofs of the city are the magnificent Durham Cathedral and Castle.

The **Cathedral** is third only to Canterbury and York in ecclesiastical significance, but excels them in architectural splendour, and is the finest and grandest example of Norman architecture in Europe. This was the power base of the wealthy Prince Bishops of Durham who once exercised king-like powers in an area known as the Palatinate of Durham. The powers vested in them by William I permitted them to administer civil and criminal law, issue pardons, hold their own parliament, mint their own money, create baronetcies, and give market charters. They could even raise their own army. Though these powers were never exercised in later years, they continued in theory right up until 1836, when the last of the Prince Bishops, Bishop William Van Mildert, died. The Palatinate Courts, however, were only abolished in 1971. It is little wonder that the County Council now proudly presents the county to visitors as 'the Land of the Prince Bishops'.

The Cathedral owes its origin to the monks of Lindisfarne, who, in AD 875, fled from Viking attacks, taking with them the coffin of St Cuthbert, shepherd saint of Northumbria. In AD 883 they settled at Chester-le-Street. However, further Viking raids in AD 980 caused them to move once more, and they eventually arrived at a more easily defended site about ten miles to the south, where the River Wear makes a wide loop round a rocky outcrop. Here, in Durham, they built the 'White Church', where St Cuthbert's remains were finally laid to rest.

The present building was begun by William de St Carileph or St Calais, Bishop of Durham from 1081 to 1096. William arrived at the White Church, bringing with him holy relics and a group of monks and scholars from Monkwearmouth and Jarrow. Forced to flee to Normandy in 1088, having been accused of plotting against William Rufus, William returned in 1091 after a pardon, determined to replace the little church with a building of the size and style of the splendid new churches he saw being built in France at that time. In August 1093 the foundation stones were laid, witnessed by King Malcolm III of Scotland, famed as the soldier who slew Macbeth in battle.

The main part of the great building was erected in a mere 40 years, but over ensuing centuries each generation has added magnificent work and detail of its own, such as the 14th century Episcopal Throne, said to be the highest in Christendom, and the Neville Screen made from creamy marble. On the North Door is a replica of the 12th century Sanctuary knocker used by fugitives seeking a haven. They were allowed to remain within the church for 37 days, after which time, if they had failed to settle their affairs, they were given a safe passage to the coast carrying a cross and wearing a distinctive costume.

Nothing is more moving, however, than the simple fragments of carved wood which survive from St Cuthbert's coffin, made for the saint's body in AD 698 and carried around the North of England by his devoted followers before being laid to rest in the mighty Cathedral. The fragments are now kept in the **Treasures of St Cuthbert Exhibition**, within the Cathedral, with examples of the Prince Bishops' own silver coins. In recognition of the renewed interest

in the life of St Cuthbert, the Cathedral is now officially called the Cathedral Church of Christ, the Blessed Mary the Virgin and St Cuthbert of Durham. **Sacred Journey**, at the Gala Theatre in Millennium Place, is a spectacular Giant Screen tourist attraction telling the story of the city and the life and death of St Cuthbert.

The Cathedral and its neighbour Durham Castle are now a World Heritage Site. **Durham Castle**, sharing the same rocky peninsula and standing close to the cathedral, was founded in 1072 and belonged to the Prince Bishops. Such was the impregnability of the site that Durham was one of the few towns in Northumbria that was never captured by the Scots. Among the motte-and-bailey castle's most impressive features are the Chapel, dating from 1080, and the Great Hall, which was built in the middle of the 13th century. The 18th century gatehouse has a Norman core, as does the massive keep, which was rebuilt in Victorian times.

Only open to the public at limited times (Tel: 0191 334 4106), the Castle is now used as a hall of residence for the students of Durham University, and The Great Hall serves as the Dining Hall of University College. But students and visitors should beware - the castle is reputedly haunted by no less than three ghosts. One is said to be of Jane, wife of Bishop Van Mildert, and takes the form of the top half of a woman in 19th-century dress. She glides along the

3   DURHAM CATHEDRAL

Durham

In 1093 work began on a magnificent cathedral to house the shrine of St. Cuthbert. The original rib vaulted church, and architectural innovation of great importance, took 40 years to build.

 see page 90

•

Durham Cathedral contains the tomb of the Venerable Bede (AD 673-735), saint, scholar-monk and Britain's first pre-eminent historian. Bede spent most of his life teaching at Jarrow and was originally buried there. His body found its final resting place in the galilee of the Cathedral in 1370.

•

4   DURHAM CASTLE

Durham

In 1069, three years after landing in Britain, William the Conqueror finally subdued the North of England.

 see page 90

On the western outskirts of Durham, straddling the A167, is the site of the Battle of Neville's Cross, fought in 1346 between Scotland and England. The Scottish army was heavily defeated and the Scottish king, David II, was taken prisoner.

5 CROOK HALL AND GARDENS

Durham

Described by Alan Titchmarsh as 'a tapestry of colourful blooms' Crook Hall is a beautiful medieval manor house surrounded by romantic gardens which include ancient fruit trees and climbing roses.

 see page 91

Norman Gallery, leaving the scent of apple blossom in her wake. A second spirit is of university tutor Frederick Copeman, who, in 1880, threw himself off the tower of the Cathedral. His ghost is said to haunt his former room off the Norman Gallery. A further apparition, who has been seen at various locations within the castle, is a cowled monk.

The university, England's third oldest after Oxford and Cambridge - was founded in 1832 by Bishop Van Mildert. In 1837 it moved into Durham Castle, though today its many buildings are scattered throughout the south of the city. The importance of the whole area surrounding the Cathedral and Castle was recognised in 1987, when it was designated a UNESCO World Heritage Site.

A favourite walk past the site starts at Framwellgate Bridge or Elvet Bridge and follows the footpaths that run through the woodlands on each bank of the River Wear, around the great loop. The path along the inside of the loop goes past The Old Fulling Mill, situated below the Cathedral, which now houses the **University of Durham Museum of Archaeology** containing material from excavations in and around the city. Prebends Bridge offers spectacular views of the Cathedral. If walking isn't your taste you can take a cruise along the river from Elvet Bridge.

The rest of Durham reflects the long history of the Castle and Cathedral it served. There are winding streets, such as Saddler Street and Silver Street (whose names attest to their medieval origin), the ancient Market Place, elegant Georgian houses - particularly around South Bailey, and quiet courtyards and alleyways. Much of Durham's shopping area is closed to traffic, making for a more relaxed atmosphere (in October 2001 Durham introduced the UK's first congestion charge). There are several churches worth visiting, including St Nicholas's Church in the Market Place, St Mary le Bow Church in North Bailey, which houses the **Durham Heritage Centre and Museum**, and St Oswald's Church in Church Street. Their presence highlights the fact that in medieval times this was a great place of pilgrimage.

The **Durham Light Infantry Museum and Durham Art Gallery** at Aykley Heads tells the story of the county's own regiment, which was founded in 1758 and lasted right up until 1968. The horrors of the First World War are shown, as is a reconstruction of a Durham street during the Second World War. Individual acts of bravery are also remembered, such as the story of Adam Wakenshaw, the youngest of a family of 13, who refused to leave his comrades after his arm was blown off. He died in action, and was awarded a Victoria Cross. The art gallery has a changing exhibition of paintings and sculpture.

The **Durham University Oriental Museum** houses a collection of Oriental art of great importance, with exhibits from ancient Egypt, Tibet, India, China, Persia and Japan. Located in parkland off Elvet Hill Road to the south of the city, the museum entrance is guarded by two stately Chinese lion-dogs.

The university also runs the 18-acre **Botanical Garden**, on Hollingside Lane (off the A167) on the south side of the city. Presenting a whistle-stop world plant tour, the gardens house rare and exotic plants from North America, Japan, South Africa, Australia and the Himalayas. A large collection of North American trees includes junior-sized giant redwoods, and in the fossil fern bed ferns and horsetails grow around the 310-year-old fossilized stem of their local ancestor *Cordaites*. Two display greenhouses with trees and plants from all over the world feature cacti and a tropical 'jungle'. The Botanic Garden is filled with some sensations of the gardening world; the Japanese Katsura tree smells of burnt sugar or candyfloss for a week every autumn, after the leaves turn yellow. The gardens, visitor centre, plant sales and glasshouses are open all year. Tel: 0191 3345521.

Crook Hall and its Gardens in Frankland Lane, close to the River Wear, offer many delights, including the Secret Walled Gardens, the Shakespeare Gardens, the Cathedral Garden and the Silver & White Garden, an orchard and a maze. The medieval manor house, one of the oldest inhabited houses in

Durham City, has a Jacobean Room haunted by the White Lady. Call 0191 384 8028 for opening times.

AROUND DURHAM CITY

FINCHALE PRIORY

4 miles N of Durham off the A167

On a minor road off the A167 lies 13th century **Finchale Priory** (pronounced Finkle). It was built by the monks of Durham Cathedral as a holiday retreat on the site of a hermitage founded by St Godric in about 1115. The ruins sit on a loop of the Wear in a beautiful location,

Finchale Priory

6 OLD MILL

Metal Bridge

Visit County Durham and fall in love with everything Durham while staying at The Old Mill where value and quality go hand in hand.

🍴 🛏 see page 91

7 THE BLUE HOUSE PUB & RESTAURANT

Haswell, nr Durham

A fine family-run country pub offering outstanding hospitality and excellent food and drink. B&B rooms coming.

🍴 see page 92

across the river from Cocken Wood Picnic Area, which is linked to the Priory by a bridge.

LANCHESTER

8 miles NW of Durham on the A691

Lanchester owes its name to the Roman fort of Longovicium ('The Long Fort'), which stood on a hilltop half a mile to the southwest. The fort was built to guard Dere Street, the Roman road that linked York and the north. The scant remains sit on private land, however, and can't be visited. Stone from the fort was used in the mostly-Norman All Saints Church, and Roman pillars can be seen supporting the north aisle. There is also a Roman altar in the south porch and some superb 12th century carvings over the vestry door in the chancel.

The area to the south of Lanchester was a typical County Durham mining area, with several small colliery villages such as Quebec, Esh Winning, Tow Law and Cornsay Colliery. A place definitely worth visiting near Lanchester is **Hall Hill Farm**, on the B6290 four miles southwest of the village. It's a real working farm, open all year to the public.

BRANCEPETH

4 miles SW of Durham on the A690

Brancepeth is a small estate village built by Matthew Russell in the early 19th century, with picturesque Georgian cottages and an 18th century rectory. To the south, in parkland, is the imposing Brancepeth Castle. The original

13th century castle was owned by the Nevills, Earls of Westmorland, and was for many years the headquarters of the Durham Light Infantry.

Close to the castle are the remains of **St Brandon's Church**. In 1998 a fire destroyed everything but the four walls and tower of what was once a beautiful and historic building. The church's magnificent woodwork, commissioned by its rector John Cosin in the early 17th century, was completely destroyed. Cosin went on to become Bishop of Durham, and restored many churches in the county. Thanks to an appeal, work is under way to restore the church.

PITTINGTON

3 miles E of Durham off the B1283

A small village, Pittington contains one of County Durham's hidden gems - the Saxon-Norman St Laurence's Church at Hallgarth. The present church dates from the 11th century, on the site of what is believed to be an even earlier Saxon church. The 12th century paintings of St Cuthbert are well worth seeing.

BISHOP AUCKLAND

Bishop Auckland is an ancient town, standing on what was Dere Street - an old Roman road. Like many County Durham towns, it owed its later prosperity to coal mining. When the surrounding pits closed, the town went into decline, but it is now gradually rediscovering itself as new industries are established. As its name implies, this was part of the territory of the Prince Bishops of Durham, who controlled what was then a scattering of small villages. Rapid expansion occurred during the 19th century and Bishop Auckland became an important market town and administrative centre for the region.

Auckland Castle, at one time the principal country residence of the Prince Bishops, is now the official residence of the Bishop of Durham. The castle began as a small 12th century manor house and over the years successive bishops have added to it; looking at it today, it appears largely 17th or 18th century. But the fabric is still basically medieval, although parts of it were destroyed during the Civil War, when it was the headquarters of Sir Arthur Hazlerigg, Governor of the North. Bishop Cosin set about making it windproof and watertight after the Restoration, turning the Great Hall into a magnificent private chapel in 1665. Dedicated to St Peter, it is reputed to be the largest private chapel in Europe. Tel: 01388 601627.

A market has been held in Bishop Auckland for centuries. Opposite the present market place is the imposing Franco-Flemish Bishop Auckland Town Hall, built in the early 1860s.

While the villages immediately

Bishop Auckland Castle

surrounding Bishop Auckland are mainly industrial, there are still some attractions worth seeing. At South Church is the cathedralesque St Andrew's Church, 157 feet long and said to be the largest parish church in the county.

AROUND BISHOP AUCKLAND

BINCHESTER

1 mile N of Bishop Auckland off the A689

Binchester Roman Fort, known to the Romans as Vinovia, was built in around AD 80. It was one of a chain of forts built along Dere Street, and has the best preserved Roman military bathhouse in Britain, complete with a pillared hypocaust heating system. In addition to acting as a military centre controlling the local area, the fort also provided a stopping-off place for troops and supplies heading towards Hadrian's Wall. A portion of Dere Street has been preserved here.

•

On display in a working men's club at West Auckland can be seen the most unlikely of trophies – the World Cup, no less. In 1910 the village's football team headed off to Italy to represent England in the first ever 'World Cup'. The team competed against teams from Germany, Italy and Switzerland, and won the Cup by beating Juventus 2-0 in the final. The team returned the following year to defend its title, and again won the trophy, which earned it the right to retain it for all time. Sadly, the trophy on show is a replica, the original having been stolen.

•

Escomb Saxon Church

hillside terraces of the village of Witton-le-Wear, noted for its handsome green, its open views, attractive cottages and a pele tower attached to fragments of a medieval manor house in the High Street. **Low Barns Nature Reserve** is a 40-hectare reserve with a nature trail, bird hides, observatory, woodland, ponds, meadow, lakes and river. The Nature Reserve and Visitor Centre are in the care of the Durham Wildlife Trust.

CROOK

5 miles NW of Bishop Auckland on the A689

Crook is a small, spacious, town with a wide square, which, in summer, is full of flowers. At one time it was a centre of coal mining, and the quaintly named Billy Row to the north of the town centre is a typical coalfield hamlet of miners' cottages.

STAINDROP

7 miles SW of Bishop Auckland on the A688

Set in a magnificent 200-acre deer park on the outskirts of the village, **Raby Castle** is one of the country's finest medieval castles - a romantic, fairy-tale building, which was once the home of the powerful Nevill family. Built in the 14th century, it houses a fine art collection and sumptuous interiors. In the 16th century over 700 barons assembled in the great Baron's Hall to plot the overthrow of Elizabeth 1 – an action which was to cost the Nevill family dearly, for it resulted in the castle and all the Nevill estates being seized by the Crown. In 1626 the castle was

---

8 THE BROWN TROUT

Sunnybrow, Crook

A friendly welcome, well-kept beers and good conversation await visitors to this Victorian village inn.

🍴 *see page 93*

---

9 THE NEW INN

Willington, nr Crook

A favourite watering hole for locals and passing motorists. Food Sunday lunchtime.

🍴 *see page 93*

ESCOMB

2 miles NW of Bishop Auckland off the A688

In the small village of Escomb is one of the true hidden gems of County Durham – the 7th century **Church of St John the Evangelist**, built using stone from nearby Binchester Roman Fort. This is one of only three complete Saxon churches in Britain, and is typically Saxon in layout, with its long, high nave and tiny chancel arch. In the south wall of the nave is a curious sundial surrounded by serpents and surmounted by what may be a mythical beast. This church is one of Northern Europe's finest examples of early Christian architecture.

WITTON-LE-WEAR

4 miles NW of Bishop Auckland off the A68

Overlooking the River Wear are the

leased to Sir Henry Vane, James 1's Secretary of State, and has remained with the Vane family ever since. The castle was besieged during the Civil War, but luckily survived and remains an impressive example of defensive and domestic architecture. Much of the interior is now Georgian and Victorian, although the Great Kitchen remains virtually unaltered since its construction over 600 years ago. The Castle, the beautiful walled garden and the coach house are all open to the public. Tel: 01833 660202

Staindrop itself is a delightful, very typical, Durham village with a long village green lined with Georgian houses. St Mary's Church, with its Saxon core, houses tombs of the Nevill and Vane families.

SHILDON

2 miles SE of Bishop Auckland on the B6282

Timothy Hackworth served from 1825 as the resident engineer on the Stockton to Darlington Railway. In 1840 he resigned and left in order to develop the Soho Engine Works at Shildon, and make his own locomotives. The first trains to run in Russia and Nova Scotia were built here. Today the Engine Works, plus his house, form **Locomotion: The National Railway Museum**. The displays, including 60 vehicles and a workshop, give a fascinating insight into the early days of rail and steam power in England. Among the main attractions is a full-size replica of the *Sans Pareil* locomotive, built by Hackworth in 1829 for the Rainhill Trials on the Liverpool to Manchester railways. Tel: 01388 772000.

It was at Shildon, in September 1825, that *Locomotion No 1* was attached to 12 coal wagons, 21 wagons with seats and a passenger coach named *Experiment*. With George Stephenson on the footplate, and a signalman riding ahead, the train carried nearly 600 passengers at 12 mph on the historic run from Darlington to Stockton (see also under Darlington).

HARTLEPOOL

There are really two Hartlepools - the old town on the headland, and the newer part with the marina and town centre, formerly known as West Hartlepool. A proud maritime town, the old part of Hartlepool dates back centuries. In the Middle Ages it was the only port within County Durham that was allowed to trade outside the Palatinate, thus confirming its importance. After

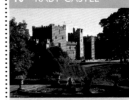

10 RABY CASTLE

Staindrop

A fascinating insight into the early days of rail and steam power, including many original exhibits.

🏛 see page 94

11 CARRSIDES FARM

Rushyford

Quiet, comfortable self-catering accommodation on a farm a short drive from the A1(M).

🛏 see page 95

Timothy Hackworth Railway Museum, Shildon

Hartlepool Marina

 12 HARTLEPOOL HISTORIC QUAY & MUSEUM

Hartlepool

Open every day all year round and voted one of the top six Heritage & History attractions in the UK, **Hartlepool Historic Quay and Museum** is a fun day out for all the family.

🏛 see page 95

the Norman Conquest, the Bruce family, whose most notable member was Robert the Bruce, King of Scotland, acquired the town. In 1201 King John bestowed the market charter on Hartlepool and ordered that the walls be built to defend it against the marauding Scots. Today parts of the wall remain and continue to stand guard over the Headland. There is a particularly fine gatehouse, called the Sandwellgate, with solid turrets on either side. Go through the pointed archway, and you find yourself on the beach.

Built by the Bruces as a burial place, the ornate 13th century St Hilda's Church stands on the site of a monastery founded by St Aidan in AD 647. The church is dedicated to St Hilda – its most famous abbess, celebrated for her teachings and her mentoring of a poor cowherd Caedmon, now regarded as the creator of religious verse. Hilda subsequently went on

to found the great monastery at Whitby, where the Synod of Whitby was held in AD 664. The church houses a collection of religious artefacts, Saxon wall carvings and a tomb, made of Frosterley marble, believed to be that of Robert the Bruce. Parts of the cemetery were excavated in the 19th century, and some of the finds are on display in Durham and Newcastle.

Hartlepool's harbour gradually went into decline, and by the early 18th century the place was no more than a fishing village. In 1835 work started on opening up the harbour once more, and rail links were established with the coalfields. But it faced stiff competition. In 1847 work started on the West Harbour and Coal Dock, and by 1860 it was thriving with timber and shipyards. Other docks were opened and Ralph Ward Jackson, a local entrepreneur, instigated the building of a new town with streets of terraced houses to house the workers. A park with many sporting and leisure facilities named in his honour is linked by a walkway to Burn Valley Gardens, the town's central green belt.

On December 16, 1914 Hartlepool was the first town in Britain to suffer from enemy action during the First World War when it was shelled from German warships lying off the coast.

Nowadays the town is a thriving shopping centre, with some interesting tourist attractions, including **Hartlepool's Maritime Experience**. The multi-ward-winning Heritage and History attraction tells the story of life at sea in the time of Nelson, Napoleon and the Battle of Trafalgar. Grouped round the small dock are various businesses and shops, such as a printer, gunsmith, naval tailor, swordsmith and instrument maker. Visitors can also go aboard HMS *Trincomalee*, a British warship originally launched in 1817. A date for the diary for visitors to Hartlepool is August 2010, when the town hosts the final leg of the Tall Ships Race.

Next door is the **Museum of Hartlepool**, with exhibits depicting life in the town through the ages. It features tales of sea monsters and the legend of the Hartlepool monkey. Washed ashore on a piece of wreckage during the Napoleonic Wars, local fishermen, unable to understand the monkey's gibberings, presumed it to be a French spy and hanged it from a gibbet on Fish Sands. Visitors to the museum can have coffee aboard the PSS *Wingfield Castle*, an old paddle steamer.

Summerhill Visitor Centre is a 100-acre country park on the western edge of Hartlepool that has been transformed for conservation and outdoor sports.

AROUND HARTLEPOOL

SEAL SANDS
3 miles S of Hartlepool off the A689

Standing in the shadows of Hartlepool Nuclear Power Station is Seal Sands and the Teesmouth

Field Centre. Local organisations have come together to protect and enhance the marshes, tidal flats and dunes here on the north shore of the Tees estuary. The area is protected as a Nature Reserve and popular with people who come to view its large Common and Grey seal population and thousands of migratory birds.

BILLINGHAM
5 miles SW of Hartlepool, off the A19

Modern Billingham grew up as a result of the great chemical plants that surrounded the River Tees. Although the town looks modern, it is in fact an ancient place, possibly founded by Bishop Ecgred of Lindisfarne in the 9th century. **St Cuthbert's Church** has a 10th century Saxon tower, and Saxon walls survive in the nave. The chancel was rebuilt and widened in 1939 to provide for the town's growing population due to the influx of workers to the chemical plants. **Billingham Beck Valley Country Park** is a country park with wetlands, wildflower meadows and a 10-acre ecology park with a visitor centre.

ELWICK
4 miles W of Hartlepool off the A19

Elwick is a small, pretty village with patches of village green running up each side of a main street lined with neat, unassuming cottages. St Peter's Church has a nave dating from the 13th century. The chancel was rebuilt in the 17th century using materials from the previous chancel, and its tower was added on

Close by the maritime Experience in Hartlepool is Jackson's Landing, a modern shopping mall situated at the centre of Hartlepool's Marina. Hartlepool Art Gallery is housed within a beautifully restored Victorian church on Church Square. It features a collection of contemporary art and photographic exhibitions. A 100-feet viewing tower affords the visitor great views of the town. The local tourist information office is here too.

Castle Eden Dene National Nature Reserve, on the south side of Peterlee, is of national importance, being one of the largest woodlands in the North East that has not been planted or extensively altered by man. It covers 500 acres and lies in a steep-sided gorge on magnesian limestone, with a wide variety of native trees and shrubs, wild flowers, bird life and butterflies, including the Castle Eden Argus, which is found only in eastern County Durham. There is a 12-mile network of footpaths, some steep and narrow. Visitors are requested to keep to paths at all times to avoid damage. Tel: 0191 586 0004

in 1813. On either side of the chancel arch are two small Saxon carvings - possibly fragments of grave markers.

TRIMDON

9 miles W of Hartlepool on the B1278

There are three villages with the word Trimdon in their name - Trimdon Grange, Trimdon Colliery and Trimdon itself. It's a quiet village with a wide main street and the unpretentious medieval St Mary Magdalene's Church.

At Trimdon Colliery, two miles to the northeast, a great underground explosion in 1882 claimed the lives of 74 miners.

HART

2 miles NW of Hartlepool on the A179

In this quiet village stands the mother church of Hartlepool – St Mary Magdalene's Church with its varied examples of architecture. The nave is Saxon, the tower and

font are Norman and the chancel is early 19th century.

On the outer wall of the White Hart Inn is a figurehead, said to have been a relic from the Rising Sun, which was shipwrecked off Hartlepool in 1861.

PETERLEE

6 miles NW of Hartlepool off the A19

Peterlee is a new town, established in 1948 to rehouse the mining families from the colliery villages around Easington and Shotton. The town has a modern shopping centre, a tourist information office and a market. Close by is the village of Easington, whose fine old St Mary's Church sits on a low hill. The church tower is Norman, and the interior contains some examples of Cosin-style woodwork.

DARLINGTON

Darlington is an important regional centre serving the southern part of County Durham, Teesdale, the Tees valley and much of North Yorkshire. It was founded in Saxon times, and has a bustling town centre with one of the largest market places in England. On its west side are the Old Town Hall and indoor market, with an imposing Clock Tower designed by Alfred Waterhouse in 1864.

There are many fine buildings in Darlington, most notably **St Cuthbert's Church** on the east side of the market place, with its distinctive tall spire. It is almost cathedral-like in its proportions, and was built by Bishop Pudsey

Brick Sculpture of "Mallard" in Morton Park, Darlington

between 1183 and 1230 as a collegiate church. Its slender lancet windows and steep roof enhance its beauty, which has earned it the name 'The Lady of the North'.

Perhaps Darlington's greatest claim to fame lies in the role it played, with neighbouring Stockton, in the creation of the world's first commercially successful public railway, which opened in 1825. It was the Darlington Quaker and banker Edward Pease who became the main driving force behind the scheme to link the Durham coalfields with the port of Stockton.

The original Darlington Station, built in 1842, was located at North Road Station. Today it serves as the **Darlington Railway Centre and Museum** – a museum of national importance which houses relics of the pioneering Stockton and Darlington Railway. These include a replica of Stephenson's Locomotion No 1, a Stockton and Darlington first-class carriage built in 1846, a World War 11 newsstand, the Derwent, (the earliest surviving Darlington-built locomotive) and even Victorian loos. The present Darlington Station, Bank Top, was constructed at a later date as part of the East Coast line linking England with Scotland. So much early railway history is to be seen hereabouts that British Rail have named their local Bishop Auckland-Darlington-Middlesbrough line the Heritage Line.

Continuing with Darlington's railway theme, there's an unusual engine to be seen in Morton Park –

Train is a life-size brick sculpture, designed by sculptor David Mach. During the summer months you can see a floral replica of George Stephenson's Locomotion No 1 in the town centre, at the foot of Post House Wynd.

AROUND DARLINGTON

PIERCEBRIDGE

4½ miles W of Darlington on the A67

Driving past the picturesque village green of Piercebridge, most motorists will be unaware that they are passing through the centre of a once important **Roman Fort**. Piercebridge was one of a chain of forts on Dere Street, which linked the northern Roman headquarters

13 BALMORAL GUEST HOUSE

Darlington

A quiet, comfortable guest house with bedrooms ranging from singles to a family room. Excellent breakfast.

🛏 see page 95

14 LA SORRENTINA

Darlington

A lovely relaxed ambience accompanies excellent Italian cooking in the heart of Darlington.

🍴 see page 96

Roman Fort, Piercebridge

at York with the north. Other forts in the chain were located at Catterick to the south and Binchester, just outside Bishop Auckland, to the north. The remains of the fort, which are still visible today, can be dated from coin evidence to around AD 270. The site is always open and admission is free. Finds from this site are housed in the Bowes Museum at Barnard Castle.

GAINFORD

7 miles W of Darlington on the A67

Gainford village sits just north of the Tees. At its core is a jostling collection of quaint 18th and 19th century cottages and houses grouped around a village green. At the south west corner of the green is St Mary's Church - a large church, built mostly in the 12th century from stone that is believed to have come from Piercebridge Roman fort, three miles to the east. Certainly a Roman altar was found built into the tower during the restoration of 1864-65, and it can be seen in the museum of Durham Cathedral.

Gainford Hall is a large Jacobean mansion built by the Reverend John Cradock in the early 1600s. Though not open to the public, it can be viewed from the road. It's hard to believe that in the 19th century the now quiet village of Gainford was a spa, visited by people from all over the North of England. Some way away along the banks of the Tees to the west, a basin can be seen where the sulphurous waters were collected.

HEIGHINGTON

5 miles N of Darlington off the A6072

Heighington is an attractive village with neat cottages and a large green. St Michael's Church is predominantly Norman, and has a pre-Reformation oak pulpit with prayers inscribed on it for its donors, Alexander and Agnes Fletcher. About three miles west of the village, near Bolam, is the shaft of a 9th century cross known as the Leggs Cross.

SEDGEFIELD

9 miles NE of Darlington on the A689

Sedgefield, well known for its National Hunt racecourse, is a small town whose market charter was issued in 1315. The grand 15th century tower of St Edmund's Church dominates the village green and the cluster of Georgian and early Victorian houses. It is famous for its intricately carved Cosin woodwork, which was on a par with the woodwork lost when Brancepeth church was destroyed by fire in 1998. Cosin's son-in-law, Denis Granville, was rector here in the late 17th century, and it was at this time that the woodwork was installed. A wheelchair-friendly Heritage Trail takes a 1.75-mile tour of the town's major sights. **Hardwick Hall Country Park** lies to the west of the town, beyond the A177. Developed as a pleasure garden between 1748 and 1792 the gardens were all laid out and the ornamental buildings were designed by the architect James Paine. The hall is now a luxury hotel, but the recently extended park with its network of woodland walks and Gothic folly is open to the public.

MIDDLETON ST GEORGE

3 miles E of Darlington off the A67

Middleton St George is a pleasant village on the banks of the River Tees to the east of Darlington, close to Teesside International Airport - once an airfield from which British and Canadian bombers flew during World War II. St George's Church dates from the 13th century with 18th and 19th century additions, and stands away from the village among fields. Curiously, the stonework has been heavily patched with brick at some point. It is thought to have been built on the site of an old Saxon church and the Victorian pews are rather incongruous - rather more like old-fashioned waiting room seats than pews.

Near Middleton St George, the village of Middleton One Row is aptly named – it consists of a single row of Georgian cottages. The cottages were inevitably altered over the years as the arrival of the railway inspired development throughout the region.

STOCKTON-ON-TEES

9 miles E of Darlington on the A166

Stockton-on-Tees found fame with the opening of the Stockton to Darlington railway in 1825, constructed so that coal from the mines of South Durham could have access to the Tees, where it would be shipped south to London. The opening of the railways encouraged the growth of industry, and the subsequent discovery of ironstone in the Cleveland Hills in the 1850s was to transform the fortunes of the town, providing considerable wealth for many of its citizens.

In the centre of Stockton's High Street are the Old Town Hall and market cross dating from the mid 18th century, and in Theatre Yard off the High Street is the **Green Dragon Museum**, set in a former sweet factory warehouse. This lively museum features displays of local history and an excellent photographic gallery.

Stockton's redbrick parish church was completed in 1713 and is one of only a handful of Anglican churches in England without a dedication. Its official title is The Parish Church of Stockton-on-Tees, though for many years it has been informally called St Thomas's. This unofficial dedication came from a chapel of

18 NUMBER FOUR

Sedgefield

A popular teashop and patisserie in the heart of Sedgefield, offering light meals, sandwiches and much more.

see page 98

Railway Sculpture, Stockton-on-Tees

•

Stockton may no longer be a busy port, but in recent years there has been a lot of development along the banks of the Tees. The spectacular £54 million Tees Barrage, built to stop the flow of pollution from the chemical plants being carried upstream by the tides, has transformed an 11-mile stretch of river. Features include Britain's finest purpose-built White Water canoe slalom course, navigation lock, fish pass and recreation site with picnic area.

•

ease that stood on the site when Stockton was a part of the parish of Norton.

Captain James Cook is said to have served the early part of his apprenticeship in Stockton. A full-size replica of his ship, *HM Bark Endeavour* is moored at Castlegate Quay on Stockton's riverside. Alongside is the *Teesside Princess*, a river cruiser that takes visitors on a pleasure trip as far inland as Yarm, stopping at Preston Hall.

Other famous characters include John Walker, the inventor of the humble friction match, who was born in Stockton in 1781, and Thomas Sheraton, the furniture maker and designer, born here in 1751 and married in St Mary's Church, Norton. One of the town's citizens with a more unusual claim to fame was Ivy Close, who won Britain's first ever beauty contest in 1908.

Preston Hall Museum, set in 110 acres of parkland to the south of the town on the banks of the Tees, is housed in the former home of the local shipbuilder Robert Ropner. Exhibits describe how life was lived in the area at the time the Hall was built in 1825. There is a re-created period street, a fully furnished drawing room of the 1820s and a collection of arms and armoury in the cellar. The museum's most famous exhibit is *The Diceplayers*, painted by Georges de la Tour in the 17th century.

YARM

9 miles E of Darlington on the A67

Set within a loop of the River Tees, Yarm was a prosperous river port as far back as the 14th century. Its broad main street, one of the widest in England, is lined with some fine Georgian houses and coaching inns, but the bustling river traffic has gone. Standing in the centre of this elegant street is the Town Hall of 1710 with marks on its walls recording the levels of past river floods, but the town's most impressive structure is the railway viaduct with its 40 arches soaring above the rooftops and extending for almost half a mile. It was at a meeting in Yarm's George & Dragon Hotel in 1820 that plans were drawn up for the Stockton & Darlington Railway, the first of all passenger-carrying railways.

LOW DINSDALE

4 miles SE of Darlington off the A67

A visit on foot or by car to Low Dinsdale is well worth while, as the 12th century red sandstone St John the Baptist Church surrounded by copper beeches is worthy of a postcard. Opposite stands a 16th century manor house built on the site of a moated Norman manor owned by the Siward family. They later changed their name to Surtees, and became well known throughout the north.

MIDDLESBROUGH

Dominating the skyline of this busy town is the **Transporter Bridge**, opened in 1911 and the only working bridge of its kind in England. The bridge can carry nine cars or 200 people on each

Sunrise, Middlesbrough

21 DORMAN MUSEUM

Middlesbrough
The Dorman Museum re-opened on the 1st March 2003 after a three year programme of major alterations and construction.

 see page 98

crossing. Captain Cook was born in Middlesbrough in 1728, and in the **Captain Cook Birthplace Museum** in Stewart Park, Marton, visitors can chart his life story and experience life below decks in the 18th century through original objects and hands-on displays. Tel: 01642 311211. Also well worth a visit when in Middlesbrough is the **Dorman Museum**, with themed displays of natural history, social history and world cultures.

mima, Middlesbrough Institute of Modern Art, is a new gallery in the heart of Middlesbrough. mima showcases an internationally significant programme of fine art and applied art from the 19th century to the present day. Tel: 01642 726720

On the southeastern edge of Middlesbrough is the National Trust's **Ormesby Hall**, a beautiful 18th century mansion with a magnificent stable block attributed to Carr of York and a superb

model railway layout and exhibition. Tel: 01642 324188. Signed off the A19 at Acklam on the southern

Middlesbrough Institute of Modern Art

19

22 THE JET MINERS INN

Great Broughton

A charming 200-year-old inn offering a warm welcome, home-cooked food and comfortable en suite accommodation.

🍴 🛏 *see page 99*

23 RAPPS CAFÉ

Saltburn-by-the-Sea

A bright, relaxed café open all day for a variety of wholesome snacks and meals.

🍴 *see page 99*

24 THE PIE CRUST

Loftus

A bright, cheerful café/coffee shop open Monday to Saturday for a good choice of home cooking.

🍴 *see page 100*

edge of Middlesbrough, **Nature's World** is a pioneering eco-experience featuring organic demonstration and ornamental gardens, wildlife areas, ponds and hydroponicum (indoor tropical garden). The centre is powered by geothermal, solar and wind power. Tel: 01642 594895.

AROUND MIDDLESBROUGH

KIRKLEATHAM

5 miles E of Middlesbrough on the A174

Two good reasons for a visit here. **Kirkleatham Museum** is a 17th century house with exhibitions on art, coast and country, and the region's ironstone mining and iron and steel heritage, with activities for children and family groups. Tel: 01642 479500. **Kirkleatham Owl Centre** has one of the country's most important collections of owls, also falcons, buzzards, vultures, kites and caracaras. Call 01642 480512 for opening times.

GUISBOROUGH

8 miles E of Middlesbrough on the A171

The stark ruins of **Guisborough Priory** stand on an elevated site overlooked by the Cleveland Hills. Founded by the great landowner Robert de Bruis II in 1119, the monastery became one of the most powerful in Yorkshire. Much extended in 1200, and rebuilt after a fire destroyed the whole site, the estate was sold in 1540 to a Thomas Chaloner, who cannibalised much of the fabric to grace ornamental gardens at his grand mansion nearby. Nothing remains of that mansion, and of the Priory itself the great arch at the east end is the most striking survival. The grounds are a popular venue for picnics.

Guisborough Priory

REDCAR

This popular town and resort on the coast is home to the oldest lifeboat in the world, on display at the **RNLI Zetland Lifeboat Museum**. It was built in 1802 by H Greathead and stands among exhibitions on fishing history, models, photographs, paintings and cards in a handsome listed building in King Street. Tel: 01642 494311

AROUND REDCAR

SALTBURN-BY-THE-SEA

5 miles SE of Redcar on the A174

This charming seaside town (complete with a pier) at the northern end of the 36-mile Heritage Coast is largely the work of the Victorians. It stands on a cliff high above a long, sandy beach, and to transport visitors from the town to the promenade and beach the ingenious water-balanced **Inclined Tramway** was built. It is still in use, the oldest such tramway to have survived in Britain. A miniature (15" gauge) railway, first established in 1947 and run entirely by volunteers, runs from the seafront to the **Valley Gardens** and the **Woodland Centre**, set between the formal pleasure gardens and the wild natural woodland beyond. The pre-Victorian Saltburn was a notorious haunt of smugglers, and those days are brought to life in the **Saltburn Smugglers Heritage Centre**, set in old fishermens' cottages next to the Ship Inn in Old Saltburn. Tel: 01287 625252.

At Skinningrove, a few miles east of Saltburn, is the **Cleveland Ironstone Mining Museum**, where visitors can discover the special skills and customs of the miners who helped make Cleveland the most important ironstone mining district in Victorian and Edwardian England.

66 GO FISHING WITH NORTHUMBRIAN WATER

Scaling Reservoir

The lakes and reservoirs are set in some of the region's most spectacular countryside helping to make a visit to one of the waters a great day out for all the family.

 see page 122

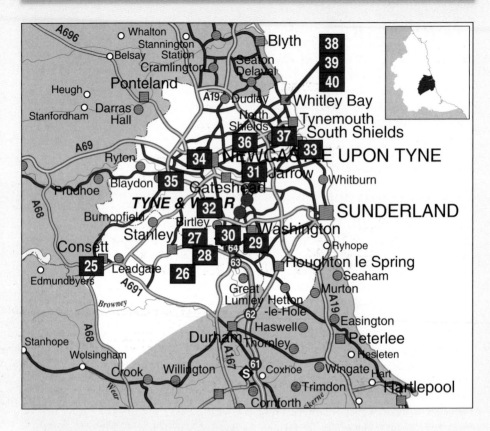

North County Durham with Tyne & Wear

The area south of the Tyne is largely industrial in character, encompassing the large towns and cities of Gateshead, Sunderland and South Shields in Tyne & Wear and, further out in County Durham, the smaller communities of Chester-le-Street and Consett. There is plenty for the visitor to see, particularly in Gateshead and Sunderland, which, like so many large British conurbations, are re-discovering themselves and their heritage. The coastline is a dramatic landscape of beaches, limestone cliffs and headlands. Awarded Heritage Coast status in 2001, a scenic attraction is the Durham Coastal Footpath - an 11-mile clifftop route from Seaham to Crimdon.

Gateshead lies immediately south of Newcastle, on the banks of the River Tyne, and in recent years both have benefited from a tremendous amount of regeneration work. In Gateshead this has revolutionised the riverside area, with such attractions as the Gateshead Millennium Bridge and Baltic Arts Centre.

To the east, South Shields is an area associated with a famous writer. The town is now well established as Catherine Cookson Country, with a Catherine Cookson Trail and a Catherine Cookson Exhibition in the local museum. The origins of Christianity can be explored in Jarrow, where the Venerable Bede lived and worked as a monk. Sunderland, to the south, is one of England's newest cities, and has the first minster to be created in England since the Reformation. Sunderland is undergoing a reformation of its own. Once an industrial centre the city is thriving again, boosted by the opening in 2002 of a link with Tyneside's Metro system. Attractions include the Sunderland Museum, with its recently refurbished Winter Gardens, and the National Glass Centre.

The area inland from the north bank of the Tyne was an important focus of the Industrial Revolution and the region is steeped in tradition and hard work. Local people – often referred to as Geordies – were employed in the coal mines, engineering works and shipyards. They didn't travel far to spend their leisure time or holidays, heading for the likes of Whitley Bay or Tynemouth, eight miles east of Newcastle city centre on the North Sea coast, but a lifetime away from their harsh living and working conditions. Today, much of that industry has now gone but the pride and passion remains, as 21st century life, leisure and industry have injected a new vibrancy in the air.

Dominating the region is Newcastle-upon-Tyne, which with Gateshead is one of Britain's most up and coming conurbations. An ambitious regeneration programme has transformed the city; stroll down Grey Street one of the most elegant streets in Europe; enjoy the view of the Tyne bridge from the Quayside; visit one of several superb museums and be sure to sample the legendary nightlife. There is a real buzz in the air. Away from Newcastle there are areas of rural calm and beauty waiting to be explored. To the west, and actually in Northumberland, stand the romantic ruins of Prudhoe Castle. One of the North East's greatest sons – George Stephenson – was born in Wylam, a village to the west of Newcastle in Northumberland. One room of the small stone cottage where he was born in 1781 is open to the public, but his story is told in greater detail in the Stephenson Railway Museum in North Shields. Legacies of the past can be explored at Segedunum Roman fort, Wallsend – so called because this was where Hadrian's Wall ended; it is now the beginning (or end) of the new Hadrian's Wall National Trail.

•

The local council at Consett has produced a small guidebook outlining various walks - none more than six and a half miles long - near the town. To the south west of Consett, almost in the North Pennines, is Allensford Park. It sits off the A 68, on the County Durham and Northumberland border, and on the banks of the Derwent. It has a picnic park, caravan site and woodland walks. Deneburn Wood, a ten acre plot of woodland with some delightful walks, also contains wood carvings by well known sculptor, David Gross.

•

25 THE CRICKETERS

nr Consett

A warm welcome, well-kept ales and Sunday roasts in a popular pub set in stunning countryside.

¶ see page 100

CONSETT

Steel-making first started in this area of County Durham at Shotley Bridge, when craftsmen from Germany set up their furnaces in the 17th century and began making swords and cutlery. When the railway came here to serve the local iron works and surrounding collieries in the 19th century, Shotley Bridge began to develop something of a reputation as a spa town, and its popularity as such is evident from the many fine houses to be seen here, such as Dial House.

Steel-making on a grand scale began in Consett in 1840, when the Derwent Iron Company built two blast furnaces. By 1890 over 7,500 people were employed in the industry, and over 1 million tonnes of steel were being produced. In the late 1960s, 6,000 people were still employed in the steelworks, though this wasn't to last. The demand for steel dropped, and in 1980 the works closed forever.

Land reclamation schemes have smartened up the area where the steelworks once stood, and its attendant spoil heaps have made way for green hillocks dotted with young trees. The countryside outside the town has some interesting places to visit.

A redundant railway line north of the town is linked to The Derwent Walk Country Park. The park covers 425 acres of woodland and riverside meadow, and the Derwent Walk itself is the track bed of the old Derwent Valley Railway between Consett and Swalwell. The main walk is 11 miles long, and suitable also for cycles, horses and wheelchairs. It gives access to a number of paths which include nature trails, the South Tyne Cycleway and the Heritage Way. Swalwell Visitor Centre, situated at the northern end of the Derwent Walk, is the starting point for a history trail and has a large pond and butterfly garden. There is another visitor's centre at Thornley Woodlands.

To the south of the town is Hownsgill Viaduct, constructed in 1857 to take the track of the Stanhope and Tyne Railway. Visitors can now walk across it, and there are some spectacular views.

AROUND CONSETT

EBCHESTER

3 miles N of Consett on the A694

Ebchester is the site of a Roman fort called Vindomora, and some scant remains can be seen in the churchyard of St Ebba's Church. It was one of a string of forts on Dere Street, the Roman road which linked York with the north. Inside the church are a number of inscribed Roman stones, including an altar to the god Jupiter, 'the greatest and the best'.

Inside Ebchester's church is the tomb of R S Surtees, creator of Jorrocks, probably the leading character in fox-hunting fiction. Surtees, born in Durham in 1805, inherited his father's Hamsterley estate in 1838, giving him the time and resources to spend his days hunting and shooting. He became High Sheriff of Durham in 1856. and died in Brighton in 1864.

CHESTER-LE-STREET

Chester-le-Street is a busy market town built around the confluence of Cong Burn and the River Wear. There was a Roman fort here at one time, and the street on which the town once stood was a Roman road, later replaced by the Great North Road.

The medieval **St Mary's and St Cuthbert's Church** is built on the site of a cathedral established in AD 883 by the monks of Lindisfarne carrying the body of St Cuthbert. His coffin rested here for 113 years until the monks took it to its final resting place at Durham. There are no fewer than 14 effigies (not all of them genuine) of members of the Lumley family within the church, though they don't mark the sites of their graves. Next to the church is the **Ankers House Museum**, situated in the medieval anchorage. Between 1383 and 1547, various anchorites, or Christian hermits, lived here.

Lumley Castle, to the east across the River Wear, was built in 1389 by Sir Ralph Lumley, whose descendant, Sir Richard Lumley, became the 1st Earl of Scarborough in the 1690's. In the early 18th century it was refashioned by the architect Vanbrugh for the 2nd Earl, and turned into a magnificent stately

Lumley Castle, Chester-le-Street

home. But gradually the castle fell out of favour with the Lumley family and they chose to stay in their estates in Yorkshire instead. For a while it was owned by Durham University before being turned into the luxurious hotel that it is today.

Waldridge Fell Country Park, two miles south-west of Chester-le-Street and close to Waldridge village, is County Durham's last surviving area of lowland heathland. A car park and signed footpaths give access to over 300 acres of open countryside, rich in natural history.

AROUND CHESTER-LE-STREET

BEAMISH

4 miles NW of Chester-le-Street on the A693

The award-winning **Beamish, The North of England Open Air Museum** is situated in 300 acres of beautiful County Durham

26 CHARLAW INN

Blackhouse, Edmondsley

A top landlord, a cheerful local clientele and good eating and drinking in a popular country pub.

 see page 101

27 PEGGY'S WICKET

Beamish

A popular dining pub serving three regularly changing real ales and a wide selection of snacks ranging from pub classics to dishes of worldwide inspiration.

 see page 102

25

28 BEAMISH MUSEUM

Beamish

An award winning open air museum illustrating life in the 1800s and 1900s

  see page 102

countryside and vividly illustrates life in the North of England in the early 1800s and 1900s. This is one of the North East's leading tourist attractions. Buildings from throughout the region have been brought to Beamish, rebuilt and furnished as they once were. Costumed staff welcome visitors and demonstrate the past way of life. Tel: 0191 370 4000.

Two miles to the northwest is **Causey Arch**, reputed to be the world's first single-arch railway bridge and in its day the longest single span bridge in England. It was designed by Ralph Wood, a local stonemason, and financed by a group of local coal owners to carry the **Tanfield Railway** - opened in 1725 - between Sunniside and Causey. In those days the wagons were pulled by horses, though steam power eventually took over. The first bridge fell down and the unfortunate designer Wood was so frightened that the second attempt would also fail that he threw himself off the bridge to his death. Steam-hauled trains now run along three miles of line between Sunniside and East Tanfield, and at Old Marley Hill are collections of locomotives and carriages and a steam-driven vintage workshop. Tel: 0191 388 7545. There's a car park and picnic area close by, and rights of way link them to Beamish.

SUNDERLAND

Sunderland's history is told in an exhibition in **Sunderland Museum** on Burdon Road (Tel: 0191 553 2323). Displays take the visitor back in time to discover the region's proud heritage in textile traditions and coal. Other exhibits include a large collection of Sunderland Pottery and a display of paintings by LS Lowry, who spent much of the last 15 years of his life in the region, finding inspiration for his work in the industrial cities and their coastline. The original **Winter Gardens**, badly damaged in the Second World war, have been re-created - a green oasis in a glass rotunda, with over 1,500 flowers and plants from all over the world. The Museum and the Winter Gardens are contained within Mowbray Park, which has been

Museum and Winter Gardens, Sunderland

fully restored with themed walkways, poetry inscriptions, historical monuments, a lake and a bowling green. The award winning **Northern Gallery for Contemporary Art** is on the top floor of the City Library and on Ryhope Road, south of the city centre, is the university-owned Vardy Art Gallery.

The **Exchange Building**, the oldest public building in the city, is a venue for the whole community to enjoy. Exhibitions, meetings and functions take place there, plus there is a restaurant and café. The famous Empire Theatre - a Sunderland institution – attracts all the top productions.

On the north side of the Wear, in the suburb of Monkwearmouth, is **St Peter's Church**, one of the most important sites of early Christianity in the country. This tiny Saxon church was founded in AD 674 by Benedict Biscop, a Northumbrian nobleman and thane of King Oswy, who had travelled to Rome and was inspired to found a monastery on his return. This was to become a great centre of culture and learning, rivalled only by Jarrow. The Venerable Bede, England's first great historian, lived and worked at St Peter's Church for a time and described the monastery's foundation in his Ecclesiastical History of England. The west tower and the wall of this most fascinating church have survived from Saxon times and the area around the church, where shipyards once stood, has been landscaped.

River Wear and "Stadium of Light", Sunderland

Close to St Peter's Church, in Liberty Way, Monkwearmouth, is the **National Glass Centre**. Glass was first made in Sunderland in the 7th century at St Peter's Church, so it's fitting that the centre was built here. Visitors can see how glass was made all those years ago, and watch modern glass blowing. There is a Glass Gallery, devoted to all forms of glass art, and in the Kaleidoscope Gallery there are several interactive exhibits showing glass's many amazing properties. Walking on the roof is not for the faint hearted, as it's made of clear glass panels 30 feet above the riverside. However, some panels are opaque, so people who don't have a head for heights can still walk there and enjoy the view. A stunning restaurant overlooks the River Wear.

Art of another kind is to be found in the St Peter's Riverside Sculpture Trail. It was established in 1990, and comprises various

Monkwearmouth Station is one of the most handsome small railway stations in the British Isles. Built in imposing neo-classical style, it looks more like a temple or a town hall. Trains no longer call here, and it has been converted into a splendid museum of the Victorian railway age. Seven new interactive galleries have been formed following a £1 million development.

works of outdoor sculpture – in metal, wood, glass and stone - placed along the banks of the Wear - mostly on the Monkwearmouth side.

Roker is one of Sunderland's suburbs, located to the north of the great breakwaters that form the city's harbour. The northern breakwater, known as Roker Pier, is 825 metres long and was opened in 1903. Roker Park, once the home of Sunderland Football Club, has been carefully restored to its former Victorian splendour, and from Roker and Seaburn through to Sunderland there is a six-mile-long seaside promenade. Crowds of people gather here in July to witness front line jet fighters and vintage planes in action during the Sunderland International Air Show. Tel: 0191 553 2000. On Old Washington Road, the **North East Aircraft Museum** houses a collection of aircraft and aero engines. The **Stadium of Light** is now the magnificent home of Sunderland FC – tours are available daily except on matchdays. Tel: 0191 551 5055. On Newcastle Road,

Fulwell Windmill is the only working windmill in the North East. Built in 1808, it has been restored to full working order and has a visitor centre. Tel: 0191 516 9790

St Andrew's Church in Talbot Road, Roker, has been described as 'The Cathedral of the Arts and Crafts Movement'. Built by E S Prior in the early 20th century, it is crammed with treasures by the leading craftsmen of the period - silver lectern, pulpit and altar furniture by Ernest Gimson, a font by Randall Wells, stained glass in the east window by H A Payne, a painted chancel ceiling by Macdonald Gill, stone tablets engraved by Eric Gill, a Burne-Jones tapestry and carpets from the William Morris workshops.

AROUND SUNDERLAND

SEAHAM

4 miles S of Sunderland on the B1287

Seaham was developed by the Marquises of Londonderry. In 1821 the family bought what was then the old village of Seaham, in order to build a harbour from which to transport coal from the family's collieries to London and the Continent. The present town grew up around the harbour, and although most of the collieries have now closed, Seaham is still very much a working town.

There is a fine sandy beach in Seaham and a sculpture trail running between the harbour and Seaham Hall celebrating the town's heritage.

Roker Lighthouse, Sunderland

A major feature of the coast is the **Durham Coastal Footpath**, an 11-mile route that runs from Seaham northwards to Crimdon. It passes through dramatic clifftop scenery and deep ravines carved into the Magnesian limestone rock.

PENSHAW

4 miles W of Sunderland off the A183

This mining village is famous for the **Penshaw Monument** - a fanciful Doric temple modelled on the Temple of Theseus, and built in 1844 in memory of John George Lambton, 1st Earl of Durham and Governor of Canada. A waymarked circular walk of just over three miles links Penshaw Monument with the River Wear.

All Saints Church dates from 1745, and has one unusual feature: inside it there is a monument to the Eliot family carved on a piece of stone from the Pyramid of Cheops in Egypt.

To the west is Lambton Castle, scene of an old tale about The Lambton Worm. Legend has it that many years ago, the heir to the Lambton estate was fishing in the Wear one Sunday morning when he should have been at worship. Instead of a fish, he caught a huge worm, which he promptly threw into a well, where it grew to an enormous size. The worm became so big that it could coil itself around hillsides, and began to terrorise the neighbourhood. Meanwhile the heir, away in the Holy Land fighting in the Crusades, knew nothing of this. On his return he met a witch who told him the secret of how the worm could be killed, on the premise that having done so he must then kill the first living thing he met on returning to his village. If he failed to do so the family would be cursed and no Lambton would die peacefully in his or her bed for nine generations. His father, hearing of this, released an old dog close by. Unfortunately, having successfully slain the worm, the young heir didn't see the old dog but his father first, he refused to kill him and the witch's prophesy about the next nine generations came true.

WASHINGTON

6 miles W of Sunderland on the A1231

Present-day Washington is a new town with modern districts scattered over a wide area surrounding the town centre. Built to attract industry into an area whose mining industry was in decline, the town has achieved its aim. Within the old village of Washington to the east of the town centre, is an attraction well worth visiting - **Washington Old Hall**, the ancestral home of the Washington family, ancestors of George Washington, the first American president.

The Hall was originally a manor house built in the 12th century for the de Wessington family, whose descendants through a female line finally left the house in 1613, when it was acquired by the Bishop of Durham.

The present Washington Old hall, in local sandstone, was rebuilt on the medieval foundations in about 1623. In 1936 it was to be

•

All that now remains of the original village of Seaham is St Mary the Virgin Church (some parts of which date from Saxon times), its vicarage, and Seaham Hall on the northern outskirts of the town. This was once the home of the Milbanke family, where in 1815 Lord Byron met and married Anne Isabella Milbanke - a marriage that was to last for only one year.

•

Washington

WWT Washington is one of nine Centres run by the Wildfowl & Wetlands Trust, a registered charity.

 see page 103

Gateshead

Enjoy that re-assuring 'home-from-home' feeling at the all-new Bowes Incline Hotel.

 see page 103

demolished, but a hastily formed preservation committee managed to save it, thanks to money from across the Atlantic. In 1955 it was officially reopened by the American Ambassador, and two years later it was acquired by the National Trust. The interiors re-create a typical manor house of the 17th century, and there are some items on display which are connected to George Washington himself, though the man never visited or stayed there. A peaceful stroll can also be enjoyed in the formal Jacobean garden. Tel: 0191 416 6879

Washington is also the home to the **Washington Wetland Centre** – a conservation area and bird watchers' paradise covering some 45 hectares of wetland, woodland, ponds and lakes sloping down to the River Wear. There are over 1,000 birds representing 85 different species, including grey herons, mallard, widgeon, nene (the state bird of Hawaii), heron, Chilean flamingos, redshank and lapwing. Other attractions include wildflower meadows, dragonflies, the Close Encounter feeding area, a Discovery Centre, Waterside Café, picnic areas, gift shop and Splash Zone play area. Excellent disabled access and free wheelchair hire. Tel: 0191 416 5454

GATESHEAD

For generations Gateshead lived very much in the shadow of neighbouring Newcastle, but no longer. Today the city is at the heart of an impressive regeneration programme that has revitalised the area. In a bid hosted jointly with Newcastle, the city was shortlisted for Capital of Culture 2008, narrowly missing out to Liverpool in the final stage.

Visitors arriving in the city from the South are greeted by one of North East England's most important modern icons - **The Angel of the North**. Commissioned by Gateshead Council and created by renowned sculptor Antony Gormley, this vast and most impressive statue, made from 200 tonnes of steel, is 65 feet high and has a wingspan of 175 feet. Erected in February 1998, the statue has attracted worldwide attention.

Nowhere is the city's transformation more evident than on the Gateshead Quays, a major new arts, leisure and cultural venue on the banks of the River Tyne. One of the most spectacular attractions in Gateshead is the £21 million **Gateshead Millennium Bridge**, erected across the Tyne in 2001 and designed to take both

The Angel of the North, Gateshead

cyclists and pedestrians. A tilting mechanism enables the bridge to pivot at both ends, forming a gateway arch, underneath which ships can pass. This operation, which has been likened to a giant blinking eye, is an engineering world first for which the bridge has received many accolades. The bridge is particularly impressive at night when it is lit by a high tech, multi-colour light display.

The **Baltic Centre for Contemporary Art** is a major international centre for Contemporary art, housed in a converted 1950s grain warehouse. It is one of the largest temporary art spaces in Europe: five galleries display an ever changing programme of work from resident artists. There is also a viewing platform with spectacular views of the Tyne Bridge. Admission is free. Next to the Baltic is the open air performance square, Baltic Square, a venue for street artists and musical events.

Further along the Quayside, in a spectacular Norman Foster building, is **The Sage Gateshead** music centre. The venue boasts a 1650-seat performance hall, 450-seat secondary hall and a school of music, as well as being home to the Northern Sinfonia orchestra. It caters for all tastes – jazz, classical, folk and rock. Linking the Baltic with the Sage Gateshead is a leisure complex with an 18 screen cinema, bowling alley, nightclubs, fitness suites and restaurants.

The **Gateshead Quay Visitor Centre** is housed in the former St

Millennium Bridge, Gateshead

Mary's parish church, a grade I listed church with Norman origins. It includes a display on Gateshead's history and future development plans and a tourist information centre.

Saltwell Park is an elegant Victorian park dating back to the 13th century that has impressive floral displays. Gateshead has achieved some notable successes in Britain in Bloom competitions, and in June Gateshead Central Nursery hosts a major flower show.

The Metro Centre is an impressive shopping and leisure complex that is popular with locals and visitors to the area. Notable sons of Gateshead include Steve Cram and Paul Gascoigne.

AROUND GATESHEAD

GIBSIDE CHAPEL

6 miles SW of Gateshead on the A694

The large mansion at Gibside Estate was owned by the Bowes

•

Shipley Art Gallery in Gateshead first opened to the public in 1917 and houses a nationally renowned collection of contemporary craft. Also on display is William C Irving's painting of the Blaydon Races. The song of the same name, written by Geordie Ridley, a Victorian music hall singer, has become the folklore anthem of Tyneside. When the painting was first exhibited, in the window of an art dealer's shop in Newcastle, it drew such crowds that the police were forced to ask the dealer to draw the blinds.

•

family, and partially demolished in 1958. Now the place is chiefly visited for the Palladian Gibside Chapel, owned by the National Trust. Building work began in the 18th century but it wasn't until 1812 that the chapel was finally consecrated.

A stately building, looking more like a small mansion than a church, Gibside was built for Sir George Bowes, whose mausoleum lies beneath it. For viewing times call 01207 541820. The Georgian Gardens, designed by Capability Brown, have miles of walks through the wooded slopes and riverside of the Derwent Valley. At nearby Rowlands Gill is the **Derwent Walk Country Park** with woodlands, riverside meadows, the Derwent Walk and the Northern Kites project.

SPRINGWELL

3 miles S of Gateshead on the B1288

Springwell is home to the **Bowes Railway**, once a private rail system pulling coal-filled wagons from pit to port. The original wagonways would have been made of wood, with horses pulling the wagons. The line finally closed in 1974, and today the site is a Scheduled Industrial Monument, the only one of its type in the country. The railway is home to a magnificent collection of around 80 colliery wagons, many of them actual Bowes Railway stock, including some former Stockton & Darlington wagons bought secondhand from the North Eastern Railway.

Many of the buildings of the original Springwell Colliery have been retained, as well as the hauliers' houses at Blackham's Hill, where there are demonstrations of the only preserved working inclines in the country, designed and built by George Stephenson. The railway organises special events and open days, and a passenger service operates between the museum centre at Springwell and Wrekenton, with an intermediate stop at Blackham's Hill. Tel: 0191 416 1847

JARROW

4 miles E of Gateshead on the A184/A194

Mixed memories surround the town of Jarrow. Once a thriving centre for the Tyneside shipbuilding industry, it gained fame during the famous Jarrow Hunger March when hundreds of unemployed men from the area walked to London to draw attention to their plight. A bas-relief at the Metro Station commemorates the event, which took place in 1936, as does a sculpture outside Morrison's Supermarket.

At Church Bank, **Bede's World** (Tel: 0191 489 2106) is a museum and outdoor interpretation centre where visitors can discover the exciting early medieval world of the Venerable Bede. It encompasses both a monastery and a church founded in the 7th century and dedicated to St Paul. The original dedication stone can still be seen within its chancel, together with fragments of Anglo-Saxon stained glass – shown to be the oldest ecclesiastical stained glass in Europe, if not the world. It was at Jarrow monastery that Bede wrote his *Ecclesiastical History of England*. He was undoubtedly Britain's first genuine historian, employing methods of checking and double checking his information that are still in use today. Jarrow Hall, a Georgian building incorporated into the museum, contains a re-created Anglo-Saxon farm.

MARSDEN

9 miles E of Gateshead on the A183

The coast between South Shields and Roker is magnificent, with rocky cliffs projecting into the sea at Lizard Point and the impressive Marsden Bay. Marsden Rock was once a famous County Durham landmark - a rock formation shaped like the Arc de Triomphe that stood in the bay. In 1996, however, it finally succumbed to the forces of nature and collapsed, leaving two tall stumps. The smaller stump proved so unstable that in 1997 it was demolished. The Rock has a famous bird colony of kittiwakes and cormorants. The caves, which were once home to smugglers, have been transformed into a bar and restaurant.

Souter Lighthouse at Lizard Point was built in 1871, and was the first reliable electric lighthouse in the world. It's a perfect example of Victorian technology, and features an engine room, foghorns and lighthouse keeper's living quarters. Owned by the National Trust, and open to the public. Tel: 0191 529 3161. **The Leas**, in the

Souter Lighthouse, Marsden

care of the Trust, is a 2½-mile stretch of spectacular coastline running from Trow Rocks to Lizard Point; it includes Marsden Bay, Marsden Rock and many grottoes and sea stacks.

SOUTH SHIELDS

8 miles E of Gateshead on the A184/A194

South Shields stretches out along the southern shore of the Tyne estuary. Though close to Newcastle and Gateshead, the North Sea coastline here is remarkably unspoiled, and can be walked along for many miles. No less a personage than King George V declared that the beach at South Shields was the finest he had seen. This is a stretch of fine firm sand, behind which a small but pleasant resort thrives.

However, it is the older part of South Shields that has given the town a new claim to fame, thanks to the work of one of the world's most popular novelists - Dame

33 ARBEIA ROMAN FORT & MUSEUM

South Shields

Built around AD160, **Arbeia Roman Fort** once guarded the entrance to the River Tyne, playing an essential role in the mighty frontier system.

 see page 105

In Baring Street, South Shields, you can see the extensive remains of the 2nd century Roman fort, Arbeia. The West Gate has been faithfully reconstructed to match what experts believe to be its original appearance, with two three-storey towers, two gates and side walls. It is the biggest reconstruction of its kind in the country, and a truly magnificent achievement. It also incorporates the Commander's Accommodation and Barracks.

Catherine Cookson, who died in 1998. She was born Katie McMullen in 1906, in a house in Leam Lane amid poverty and squalor, the illegitimate child of a woman called Kate Fawcett. The house is gone now, but a plaque has been erected marking the spot.

Catherine Cookson wrote a series of best-selling novels which captured the world of her own childhood, and that of her parents and grandparents, with vivid clarity. It was a world that was shaped in the 19th century around the narrow streets and coal mines - a world of class warfare and conflict, passion and tragedy, violence and reconciliation.

A **Catherine Cookson Trail** has been laid out in the town, showing places associated with her and her books, and a leaflet is available to guide you round. The South Shields Museum, which recently underwent a major redevelopment, includes an

enhanced Catherine Cookson's gallery and an Arts Adventure Centre.

Much of the old harbour at South Shields has been restored, particularly around the Mill Dam which is home to the Customs House offering a cinema, theatre, art galleries and an excellent Italian restaurant. Fine Georgian buildings and warehouses still survive in this area along the riverside.

NEWCASTLE-UPON-TYNE

Newcastle, the region's capital, is rapidly becoming one of Britain's most exciting cities, and contains many magnificent public buildings and churches. Situated above the River Tyne, it is linked to its neighbour Gateshead as one visitor destination.

The **Tyne Bridge** has long been the icon by which Newcastle is internationally known. Opened in 1928, it bears an uncanny resemblance to the Sydney Harbour Bridge, which isn't surprising as both were designed by the same civil engineering company. The bridge is the start point of the world's biggest half marathon: on Sunday, October 5th, 2008, some 50,000 will cross the bridge before running, jogging or walking their way to the seaside finish at South Shields.

Newcastle has enjoyed a varied and colourful history and in its time has acted as a Roman frontier station, a medieval fortress town, an ecclesiastical centre, a great port, a

St Peters Basin, Newcastle-upon-Tyne

mining, engineering and shipbuilding centre and a focal point of the Industrial Revolution that was to change the face of the world.

The **Quayside** is the first view of Newcastle for visitors from the south, whether travelling by road or rail. The area is the symbolic and historic heart of this elegant city and boasts some 17th-century merchants' houses mingling with Georgian architecture, and the beautiful Guildhall contains a state of the art visitor information centre. It has been a focal point for activity since the first bridge was built across the river in Roman times and has been revitalised in recent years with some sensitive and imaginative restoration of the river front area. There are now a number of lively cafés and wine bars along with a regular Sunday market.

To the west of the Quayside is Central Station, designed by local architect John Dobson and officially opened by Queen Victoria in 1850.

The city centre is compact, lying mostly within a square mile, so it is easy and rewarding to explore on foot. For the most part the streets are wide and spacious, and like the later Quayside developments after the great fire of 1855, much of the architecture is in the Classical style. During the 17th and early 18th centuries, Newcastle was a major coal port, with its core - still basically medieval in layout - near the riverside. But by the late 1700s the city began moving north,

and in the early 1800s architects like William Newton, John Stokoe and John Dobson began designing some elegant Georgian buildings and spacious squares.

Grey's Monument, an 18th century landmark dedicated to the former Prime Minister Earl Grey, stands at the head of Grey Street, about which John Betjeman wrote that "not even Regent Street in London, can compare with that subtle descending curve". With over 40% of its buildings officially listed, Grey Street was awarded the title of Britain's favourite street by listeners to the Radio 4 Today programme.

The **Castle Keep** at Castle Garth was built by Henry II in the 12th century on the site of the 'new castle', built in 1080 by Robert, eldest son of William 1, on the site of the Roman fortifications of Pons Aelius. This earlier wooden castle, from which the city takes its name, is thought to have been the start of Hadrian's Wall before it was extended east. It was built after uprisings against the new Norman overlords that followed the killing of Bishop Walcher in Gateshead at a meeting to discuss local grievances.

Henry's impressive new

Grainger Town, the historic centre of Newcastle, contains many fine examples of classical Victorian architecture. It was designed by Richard Grainger from 1834 with architects John Dobson, John Wardle and George Walker. Up until recently the area was in a state of physical and economic decline but it has been restored to its former splendour by the Grainger Town Project, just one of the examples that epitomises the renaissance of the city. Of particular interest is the Edwardian Central Arcade with its mosaic paving.

Castle Keep, Newcastle-upon-Tyne

34 DISCOVERY
MUSEUM

Newcastle upon Tyne

Discovery is the North East of England's most popular free museum.

see page 105

•

On New Bridge Street, the Laing Art Gallery has been attracting visitors for over a hundred years. The permanent collection includes beautiful 18th and 19th century paintings and world-renowned watercolours. The gallery also displays contemporary artwork and has initiated a national competition, Laing Solo, to showcase emerging artists. Tel: 0191 232 7734. Outside the gallery is the Blue Carpet, a pedestrian square constructed from purpose-made blue glass tiles.

•

structure was built entirely of stone, and reached 100 feet in height. Although the battlements and turrets were added in the 19th century, much of it is Norman. The only other remaining castle building is Black Gate, dating back to 1247. If at first glance the structure looks a little unusual, it is because of the house built on top of it in the 17th century. The castle was in use during the Civil War, when it was taken by the Scottish army after the Royalist defeat at the Battle of Newburn, five miles west of Newcastle, in 1640.

Many of the other medieval buildings were demolished in the mid-19th century to make way for the railway, and the Castle and Black Gate were fortunate to survive.

At one time, Newcastle was surrounded by stout walls that were 20 to 30 feet high in places and seven feet thick. Parts of these survive and include a number of small towers, which were built at regular intervals. Begun in 1265, the walls were eventually completed in the mid-14th century. They were described as having a "strength and magnificence" which "far passeth all the walls of the cities of England and most of the cities of Europe". The best remaining sections are the West Walls behind Stowell Street, and the area between Forth Street and Hanover Street, south of Central Station, which leads to spectacular views of the River Tyne from the gardens perched on the cliff side.

One unusual feature of the walls was that they passed right

through the grounds of a 13th century Dominican monastery, known as Blackfriars, causing the prior to protest loudly. To keep the peace, a door was cut through to allow the monks access to their orchards and gardens. Blackfriars was later converted and turned into almshouses for the destitute. Earmarked for demolition in the 1960s, the building was eventually saved. The church is long gone, but the remaining buildings have been renovated and opened as a craft centre and restaurant grouped around a small square. It's another of the area's hidden places, and well worth a visit.

Newcastle has two cathedrals - the Anglican **St Nicholas's Cathedral** on St Nicholas Street, and the Roman Catholic **St Mary's Cathedral** on Clayton West Street. St Nicholas, dating from the 14th and 15th centuries, was formerly the city's parish church, and it still has the feel of an intimate parish church about it. Built in 1844, St Mary's was one of A W H Pugin's major works; the spire he originally designed was never built, and the present one dates from 1872.

This is a metropolitan city of great vibrancy and activity, and there's plenty to do, with a rich variety of entertainment on offer. There is a choice of theatres, cinemas, concert venues and an opera house.

The city boasts a wide range of museums and art galleries: The **Discovery Museum**, Blandford Square, depicting Newcastle's social and industrial past; the **Hancock**

Museum, Barras Bridge - the region's premier Natural History museum, with a magnificent collection of birds, mammals, insects, fossils and minerals; the **Life Science Centre**, Times Square – genetic science brought to life; the **Hatton Gallery**, Newcastle University Art Dept – a permanent collection of West African sculpture; the **Museum of Antiquities**, King's Road; the **Shefton Museum**, Newcastle University – Greek Art and Archaeology; the **Side Gallery**, The Side – documentary photography exhibitions; the **Military Vehicle Museum**, a collection of World War II and other vehicles housed in the only remaining pavilion of the 1929 exhibition; and the **Newburn Hall Motor Museum**, Townfield Gardens – a private collection of vintage vehicles.

Down near the quayside is a unique group of half-timbered houses known as **Bessie Surtees House**, owned by English Heritage. The rooms are richly decorated with elaborate plaster ceilings, and there is some beautiful 17th century wall panelling.

To the west of the city, on the south bank of the Tyne, is **Blaydon**, famous for its races, which inspired one of Newcastle's anthems, *The Blaydon Races*. But horse racing hasn't been held here since 1916, and the racecourse is no more. Gosforth Park, to the north of the city, is where horse racing now takes place (Tel: 0191 222 7849 for details of race days). Near Blaydon is the Path

Head Water Mill, a restored 18th century mill.

Newcastle is a true Northern capital – a proud city that doesn't look to the South for inspiration and guidance. There is an unmistakable air of confidence in the future. Along with neighbouring Gateshead, Newcastle staged a bid to become European City of Culture 2008. Narrowly missing out to Liverpool in the final stages, the city has none the less been designated as a Centre of Cultural Excellence with a wide range of events planned for the coming years.

The Metro Rapid Transport System, Britain's largest after London, links Newcastle with Gateshead, South Shields, Sunderland and the northern coastal areas of Tynemouth and Whitley Bay.

NORTH AND EAST OF NEWCASTLE-UPON-TYNE

WALLSEND

3 miles E of Newcastle on the A193

In Wallsend the mighty shipyards tower over **Segedunum Roman Fort, Baths and Museum** on Buddle Street. The fort, on the banks of the River Tyne, was the last outpost on Hadrian's Wall. Segedunum (it means 'strong fort') stood at the eastern end of the Hadrian's Wall. Originally the wall only went as far as Newcastle, but it was decided to extend it to deter sea attacks. There are only scant remains of the structure in the district nowadays.

35 PATH HEAD WATER MILL

Blaydon-on-Tyne

For many years, the 18th century **Path Head Water Mill** lay abandoned and neglected. Then, in 1995, it was decided to restore it to its full working glory.

 see page 105

36 SEGEDUNUM ROMAN FORT, BATHS & MUSEUM

Wallsend

Segedunum is once again the gateway to Hadrian's Wall. It is the most excavated fort along the Wall and has a large interactive museum plus a 35 metre high viewing tower.

 see page 106

37 BELL & BUCKET

North Shields

This listed, ex fire-station is well worth a visit for anyone looking for home cooked food, real ales or just a friendly atmosphere. B&B available

🍴 🛏 *see page 106*

Segedunum is a reconstruction of what the Roman fort would have looked like. Over 600 Roman soldiers could have been garrisoned here at any one time, and the area must have been a bustling place. Now visitors can explore the reconstructed fort, get a stunning view from a 114-feet viewing tower, and watch archaeologists uncovering yet more foundations of the original wall. The reconstructed bath house is the only one of its kind in Britain.

NORTH SHIELDS

5 miles E of Newcastle on the A193

Standing at the mouth of the River Tyne the town is named after the shielings (fishermens' huts) on the riverbank. The **Fish Quay**, dating back to 1225, grew up when fishermen were called upon to supply Tynemouth Priory. While the boats are smaller in number than in its heyday the port is still a hive of activity, the best time to see fishing boats come into port and experience the hustle and bustle of the landing of catches is between 6 and 7pm. Fabulous fresh fish can be bought from the numerous fishmongers. Many of the buildings on the Fish Quay are linked to the fishing industry. The 'High' and 'Low' lights are prominent landmarks on the upper and lower banks of the Fish Quay that were designed to guide vessels entering the Tyne.

Well worth a visit in North Shields is the **Stephenson Railway Museum** in Middle Engine Lane. George Stephenson began his career as a humble engine-man at Willington Ballast Hill before moving to Killingworth, where he eventually became an engine-wright. The museum remembers the man and his achievements as well as covering steam, diesel and electric trains and explaining how trains work. Tel: 0191 200 7146. See also under Shildon and Darlington.

TYNEMOUTH, WHITLEY BAY AND CULLERCOATS

8 miles E of Newcastle on the A193

These three towns form a linked resort. Nestling at the mouth of the River Tyne, Tynemouth boasts a proud maritime heritage. In 1864 the first Volunteer Life Brigade was created here (still in operation today), and visitors can learn more about this vital service in the small museum attached to the lifeboat

Stephenson Railway Museum, North Shields

Cullercoats Bay

38 DOWN UNDER RESTAURANT

Whitley Bay

A small, cheerful restaurant right on the promenade, serving home-cooked dishes from around the world.

see page 106

39 THE LIGHTHOUSE GUEST HOUSE

Whitley Bay

A very friendly, relaxed and comfortable guest house a short walk from the golden sands of Whitley Bay.

see page 107

station. Overlooking the river is the notable **Collingwood Monument**, the grand statue of Admiral Lord Collingwood, Nelson's second-in-command at Trafalgar, who went on to win the battle after Nelson's death. The four guns below the statue are from his ship, the *Royal Sovereign*. Tynemouth Priory was built over the remains of a 7th century monastery, which was the burial place of St Oswin, King of Deira (the part of Northumbria south of the Tees), who was murdered in AD 651. The priory was as much a fortress as a monastery, which explains the existence of the adjoining 13th century castle ruins. Tynemouth station is the venue for a popular antique market held every weekend. The Palace building on Grand Parade at Tynemouth is home to the **Childhood Memories Toy Museum**, where over 4,000 toys are on display. Tel: 0191 259 1776

Long Sands is an award winning and gloriously sandy beach that stretches from Tynemouth to Cullercoats, a small town renowned for its history of salt production. In the 1700s around 2180 tons of salt were gathered here each year, abandoned caves were once the hiding place of smugglers who made their fortune illegally transporting it to Scotland. Much quieter than the neighbouring resorts of Tynemouth and North Shields, Cullercoats was a favourite retreat of the famous American artist Winslow Homer, who painted some of his finest works here.

The seaside resort of Whitley Bay has a unique atmosphere at weekends and bank holidays when young people from all over the country come to sample its legendary nightlife. The town has some excellent safe beaches and in

40 ST MARY'S LIGHTHOUSE

Whitley Bay

Just north of Whitley Bay, you'll find **St Mary's Lighthouse** and the adjoining keepers' cottages, situated on a small island which is accessible at low tide.

  see page 107

July hosts the Whitley Bay International Jazz Festival.

On a small island, easily reached on foot from Whitley bay at low tide, is **St Mary's Lighthouse**. The reward for climbing the 137 steps to the top is magnificent views of the Northumberland coast. Completed in 1898, the Lighthouse remained in operation until 1984, when it was superseded by modern navigational techniques. North Tyneside council now runs the Lighthouse and former keeper's cottages as a visitor centre and nature reserve.

SEATON SLUICE

8 miles NE of Newcastle on the A193

Inland from Seaton Sluice is **Seaton Delaval Hall**. This superb Vanburgh mansion, the ancestral home of the Delavals, was built in the Palladian style in 1718 for Admiral George Delaval. Gutted by fire in 1822, it was never restored. Tel: 0191 237 1493. In the grounds of the house stands the Norman St Mary's Chapel.

BLYTH

12 miles NE of Newcastle on the A193

Blyth is a small industrial town at the mouth of the River Blyth. Much of the town's industrial heritage is linked to the Northumberland coalfields, their rapid decline in recent years is a loss from which the area is only slowly recovering. The oldest part of the town is set around an 18th century lighthouse called the High Light. Blyth claims its own piece of railway history with one of the country's earliest wagonways, the **Plessey Wagonway**, dating from the 17th century and built to carry coal from the pits to the riverside. As well as coal mining and shipbuilding, the town was once a centre of salt production, and in 1605 it is recorded that there were eight salt pans in Blyth. Blyth's industrial landscape and coastline was the inspiration for several paintings by L S Lowry. The building that is now the headquarters of the Royal Northumberland Yacht Club was a submarine base during the Second World War.

NORTH AND WEST OF NEWCASTLE-UPON-TYNE

WYLAM

5 miles W of Newcastle off the A69

Wylam is the birthplace of George Stephenson, railway pioneer, and one room in the little stone cottage where he was born in 1781 is open to the public.

PRUDHOE

9 miles W of Newcastle on the A695

The romantic ruins of **Prudhoe Castle** are in the care of English Heritage. King William the Lion of Scotland unsuccessfully attacked the castle in 1173 and 1174, and the threat of further attacks led Henry II to agree to the building of a new stone castle. Completed in the 12th century, it was one of the finest in Northumberland, and was later provided with a moat and drawbridge, a new gatehouse and a chapel. There is an impressive oriel window above the altar of the chapel. A Georgian manor house in the courtyard houses an exhibition, which tells the history of the castle. Tel: 01661 833459

MICKLEY

10 miles W of Newcastle on the A695

A signpost at Mickley Square points visitors to **Cherryburn**. The house is noted as the birthplace of Thomas Bewick, the well-known illustrator and wood engraver, famous for his portrayal of birds, animals and country life. Now owned by the National Trust, the house contains an exhibition of his woodcuts and hosts regular demonstrations of the printing techniques used in his time. Tel: 01661 843276

PONTELAND

7 miles NW of Newcastle on the A696

Prudhoe Castle

Though this small town has largely become a dormitory town for Newcastle-upon-Tyne, resulting in a lot of recent development, it still retains a character of its own. **St Mary's Church**, much altered but essentially 12th century, stands opposite the attractive Blackbird Inn, housed in a 13th and 14th century fortified house. Within the gardens of the Old Vicarage is a 16th century vicar's pele.

A few miles north of Ponteland are **Kirkley Hall Gardens**, which are open to the public from 10 to 3 except weekends out of season. Tel: 01670 841200. There are 35,000 different species of labelled plants here, and it is home to the national collections of beech, dwarf willow and ivy. Other attractions include a Victorian walled garden, sunken and woodland garden, greenhouse plants and herbaceous and ornamental borders.

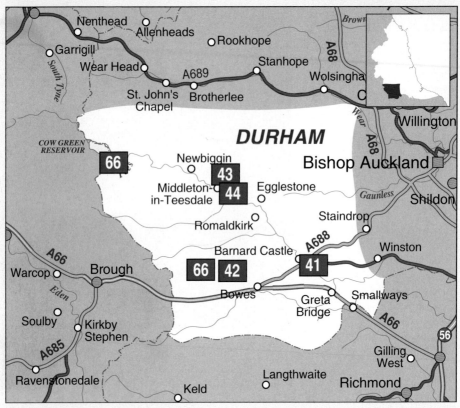

Weardale, Teesdale & the Pennines

To the west, County Durham sweeps up to the Northern Pennines – a hauntingly beautiful area of moorland, high fells and deep, green dales. Officially designated as an Area of Outstanding Natural Beauty in 1988, the North Pennines covers almost 2,000 square kilometres. It is one of the most remote and unspoiled places in the country and has been called 'England's last wilderness'.

The great northern rivers of the Wear, the Tees, the Tyne and the Derwent have their sources here. Tumbling mountain streams have cut deep into the rock, creating the impressive waterfalls of Low Force, High Force, and Cauldron Snout. These are magical places, and show just how water has shaped the Durham Dales. The area is rich in wildlife. Hen harriers, merlins and other rare species breed here, and in spring and summer the plaintive call of the curlew can be heard.

This is ideal country for walking and cycling, though in the winter months it can be wild and inhospitable. There are numerous rights-of-way to be explored, including the C2C (Coast to Coast) cycle path. The Pennine Way cuts through County Durham in the south, close to the towns of Barnard Castle and Middleton-in-Teesdale, continuing westward through Upper Teesdale until it enters Cumbria. Further north it enters Northumberland to the west of Haltwhistle and then the Northumberland National Park.

Man has left his mark here too, for this is working countryside. The lower reaches have been farmed for centuries, and the high fells are home to many flocks of sheep. At one time there were woollen mills in Barnard Castle, providing a ready market for local sheep farmers. Lead mining was a thriving industry, with mines located at Killhope, Ireshopeburn and St John's Chapel. Middleton-in-Teesdale was once the headquarters of the London Lead Company, a great Quaker business venture.

There are two great County Durham dales - Teesdale to the south and Weardale to the north. Of the two, Teesdale is the softer, particularly in its lower reaches, which share an affinity with the Yorkshire Dales. This isn't surprising, for at one time part of the River Tees formed the boundary between County Durham and Yorkshire. The lower Dale is dotted with charming villages that nestle along the bank of the River Tees, as it winds its way between the historic towns of Barnard Castle and Middleton-in-Teesdale. Small farmsteads, whitewashed in the local tradition, are surrounded by dry stone wall enclosures. Travelling up the dale the vista opens out into miles of open moorland, home to a multitude of wildlife and unique flora. Beyond Middleton-in-Teesdale the B6277 winds up and over some bleak but beautiful scenery until it arrives at Alston in Cumbria, England's highest market town.

The A689, which winds its way through Weardale further north, follows an alternative route to Alston, passing through a dale that was once the hunting ground of Durham's Prince Bishops. Life, at one time, must have been harsh here and the houses and villages seem grittier somehow than those of neighbouring Teesdale. The scars on the landscape expose the regions past as one of the most heavily industrialised upland landscapes in England. Farming developed hand in hand with mining, as the miners supported their variable income with produce from their smallholdings. Methodism was very strong within the communities and many former Methodist chapels can still be seen in the area. There is however plenty to see here, such as the lead mining museum at Killhope, the curious fossilised tree stump at Stanhope, and the village of Blanchland, a few miles to the north in Derwentdale.

43

41 BOWES MUSEUM

Barnard Castle

The Bowes Museum is one of County Durham's great surprises - a beautiful and grand French chateau-style museum on the outskirts of the historic town of Barnard Castle.

 ❙❙ *see page 108*

BARNARD CASTLE

This historic market town is a natural centre for exploring Teesdale and the Northern Pennines. Set beside the River Tees, 'Barney' is recognised nationally as one of the 51 most historically and architecturally important towns in Great Britain. The town derives its name from **Barnard Castle**, founded in the 12th century by Bernard, son of Guy de Baliol, one of the knights who fought alongside William I. The castle played an important role in the defeat of the Northern Earls who

rose against Elizabeth I in 1569. Besieged by rebel forces for 11 days, the castle was ultimately forced to surrender, but not before its resistance had provided time for Queen Elizabeth's army, under the Earl of Sussex, to speed to York and force the rebels to flee. Many were executed and those leading families who had supported the plans to overthrow Elizabeth I lost their lands.

The castle ruins, with the imposing round keep overlooking the River Tees, have a gaunt beauty. Riverside walks wind through the woods that once formed part of the castle's hunting grounds. County Bridge, a narrow arched bridge built in 1569, traverses the fast flowing River Tees close to the Castle. It formerly spanned the boundaries of two counties and the lands of two bishops, and illicit weddings were regularly conducted in the middle of the bridge, where neither bishop could object.

The town has an especially rich architectural heritage, with handsome houses, cottages, shops and inns dating from the 17th to the 19th centuries. The octagonal **Market Cross** is a most impressive building, which dates back to 1747 and has served numerous purposes such as courthouse, town hall and jail. Underneath the veranda (a later addition) a lively butter market took place. You can still see the bullet holes in the weather-vane, resulting from a wager by two local men in 1804, shooting from outside the Turk's Head, 100 yards away, to determine who was the best shot.

Barnard Castle

The building was fully restored in 1999.

A walk along Newgate will bring visitors to the **Bowes Museum**, one of County Durham's great surprises and surely one of the most spectacular buildings in England. This magnificent French-style château was the inspiration of John Bowes, son of the Earl of Strathmore, and Joséphine, his French actress wife. The designer of the Bowes building was a Frenchman, Jules Pellechet, who apparently took his inspiration from the grand Town Hall in Le Havre. The couple's love of the arts and a desire that people from all walks of life should be able to partake in such riches resulted in this superb legacy. Sadly both died before their dream could be realised, but the museum was completed and opened to the public in 1892. Today the museum, open daily at 10am, houses one of England's finest art collections including paintings by Canaletto, Goya and Turner, as well as fine textiles, ceramics, clocks and watches and antique furniture. A diverse programme of temporary exhibitions (Summer 2008 – Alfred Sisley: Impressionist Landscapes)running throughout the year complements permanent displays (Tel 01833 690606 for details). The most famous and best loved exhibit is undoubtedly the Silver Swan, a 230-year-old, beautifully crafted life-size mechanical bird that appears to pick up and swallow a fish to the backdrop of a tinkly music box. Set in 23 acres of parkland, the museum boasts a splendid parterre garden; a Tree Trail in the grounds highlights unusual trees from around the world.

AROUND BARNARD CASTLE

GRETA BRIDGE

4 miles SE of Barnard Castle on the A66

Lovers of romantic landscape should make their way south of Barnard Castle to Greta Bridge on the A66 - the graceful old bridge immortalised in paintings by great English water-colourists such as Cotman and Turner. Footpaths run by the riverside, through the edge of Rokeby Park. Close by are the ruins of medieval **Mortham Tower**, subject of Sir Walter Scott's narrative poem of colourful chivalry and courtly love, *Rokeby*.

The Bank was once Barnard Castle's main commercial street and you can still see several Victorian shop windows. Blagraves House is the oldest inhabited building and it is here that Oliver Cromwell is reputed to have sojourned in 1648. The house is now a restaurant, and the locality is an excellent centre for antiques collectors. At the bottom of the Bank glimpses of the town's industrial roots can still be found in Thorngate and Bridgegate. Weavers' cottages have been converted into modern dwellings and grassy slopes cover the remains of riverside woollen mills.

Mortham Tower, Greta Bridge

42 CLOVE LODGE

Baldersdale, Barnard Castle

A scenically located two-bedroom farmhouse cottage available for either B&B or self-catering holidays.

 see page 108

66 GO FISHING WITH NORTHUMBRIAN WATER

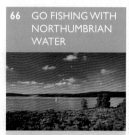

Grassholme and Hury Reservoirs

The lakes and reservoirs are set in some of the region's most spectacular countryside helping to make a visit to one of the waters a great day out for all the family.

 ⚏ see page 122

The elegant Palladian house, where Scott stayed to write his poem, is open to the public during the summer months. Charles Dickens travelled up the Great North Road from London with his illustrator Hablot K Browne to gather material for his third novel Nicholas Nickleby, and they spent their first night in Greta Bridge (see also under Bowes).

EGGLESTONE ABBEY

2 miles S of Barnard Castle, near the A66

South East of Barnard Castle the road leads over an old pack horse bridge to Egglestone Abbey. It is made up of the ruins of a Premonstratensian abbey of which most of the nave and chancel, built in the 13th and 14th century, survives. Close by is the Meeting of the Waters where the river Greta joins the River Tees, creating splendid views.

BOWES

4 miles W of Barnard Castle off the A66

The ruined Norman castle of Bowes was built on the site of a Roman fort, guarding the approach to Stainmore Pass. In 1838 Charles Dickens visited the village to collect material for *Nicholas Nickleby*, and noticed a boys' academy run by William Shaw in the main street. The school became the model for Dotheboys Hall and Shaw was immortalised as Wackford Squeers. Shaw is buried in the churchyard of St Giles' Church along with George Taylor, Dickens's inspiration for Smike. "I think," Dickens later said,

"his ghost put Smike into my head upon the spot."

Three miles west of Bowes on the A66 is the **Otter Trust's North Pennines Reserve**, a 230-acre wildlife reserve with British and Asian otters and bird hides overlooking wetland areas. The otters are fed at noon and 3pm daily. Tel: 01833 628339

ROMALDKIRK

4 miles NW of Barnard Castle on the B6277

Between Middleton and Barnard Castle, the B6277 follows the south bank of the River Tees passing through pretty unspoiled villages such as Cotherstone and Romaldkirk. The church at Romaldkirk, known as the **Cathedral of the Dales**, is dedicated to the little-known St Romald or Rumwald, son of a Northumbrian king who could miraculously speak at birth. Beautiful stone houses are set around spacious greens and there are delightful walks close to the river.

EGGLESTON

6 miles NW of Barnard Castle on the B6281

Within the grounds of Eggleston Hall are **Eggleston Hall Gardens**, which are open to the public all year. There are four acres of garden here within the high wall that once enclosed the kitchen garden. The ornamental gardens are laid out informally, with many rare herbaceous plants and shrubs to be seen. Vegetables are cultivated using the traditional organic methods. The Gardens are open all year, 10 to 5 daily.

MIDDLETON-IN-TEESDALE

10 miles NW of Barnard Castle on the B6277

Middleton-in-Teesdale, the capital of Upper Teesdale, is a small town in a dramatically beautiful setting with the River Tees running below, while all around is a great backcloth of green hills, within the North Pennines Area of Outstanding Natural Beauty. The town's links with the lead-mining industry can be seen in the Market Square, where there is a handsome cast-iron fountain which was purchased and placed there in 1877 by the employees of the Quaker-owned London Lead Mining Company. The expense was covered from subscriptions raised for the retirement of the company's local superintendent, Robert Bainbridge. At the west end of Hude is Middleton House, the company's former headquarters.

Although the lead-mining industry disappeared at the beginning of the 19th century, Middleton still retains the strong feeling of being a busy working town. The surrounding hills still bear the scars, with the remains of old workings, spoil-heaps and deep, and often dangerous, shafts. The town's agricultural links remain strong, with streets bearing names such as Market Place, Horsemarket and Seed Hill. **Meet the Middletons**, on Chapel Row, is an excellent interpretation of life in the area in the 1800s, with family-friendly interactive displays.

Like Barnard Castle, Middleton is increasing in popularity as a centre from which to explore Teesdale and the Northern Pennines. Middleton is the centre for some magnificent walks in Upper Teesdale. The most famous of these is The Pennine Way, which passes through the town on its 250-mile route from Derbyshire to Kirk

43 COUNTRY STYLE BAKERY & TEA SHOP

Middleton-in-Teesdale

Hazel prepares an excellent selection of sweet and savoury delights to enjoy throughout the daytime, seven days a week.

see page 109

44 HIGH FORCE WATERFALL

Middleton-in-Teesdale

High Force is reputed to be the highest unbroken fall of water in England.

see page 109

Upper Teesdale

66 GO FISHING WITH NORTHUMBRIAN WATER

Cow Green, Selset and Balderhead Reservoirs

The lakes and reservoirs are set in some of the region's most spectacular countryside helping to make a visit to one of the waters a great day out for all the family.

  see page 122

Low Force Waterfall, Upper Teesdale

Yetholm in Scotland. Turning west along Teesdale the track passes through flower-rich meadows, traditional, whitewashed farmsteads and spectacular, riverside scenery, including the thrilling waterfalls at Low Force, High Force and Cauldron Snout.

The majestic **High Force** is England's largest waterfall in terms of water flow, with a dramatic 21-metre drop over Great Whin Sill at the end of a wooded gorge. After heavy rainfall its rumble can be heard over a mile away. **Low Force** isn't so much a waterfall as a series of cascades, and whilst less spectacular than its upstream neighbour, it is equally beautiful. Further up the Dale from High Force is Cow Green Reservoir and below it Cauldron Snout, which

cascades down dolerite steps. A nature trail leads from Cow Green car park to Cauldron Snout and Moor House Nature Reserve, home to some rare Alpine plants, including the Blue Gentian.

About three miles northwest of Middleton-in-Teesdale, near the village of Newbiggin, is the **Bowlees Visitor Centre**, where information on the natural history and geology of the area is displayed. The picnic area has four small waterfalls and a footpath to Gibson's Cave and Summerhill Force.

HAMSTERLEY FOREST

9 miles N of Barnard Castle off the A68

Hamsterley Forest is one of the Forestry Commission's most attractive Forest Parks. This huge area encompassing over 5,500 acres of mature woodland is managed for timber production, and has 1,100 acres available for recreation. A wide range of activities are on offer for visitors including informal or guided walks, orienteering, horse-riding and cycling (bikes can be hired). There is a visitors centre with displays on forestry, wildlife and timber usage, and large, grassy areas make splendid picnic spots.

Surprisingly enough, the Forest is largely artificial and relatively recent in origin, having been planted only 40 to 50 years ago. Much of it covers areas once worked by the lead-mining industry. This is a good area to discover a range of wild flowers and, in the damper places, fungi. Red squirrels can still be seen in the forest, along with roe deer, badgers, adders and up to 40 species of birds including heron, woodcock, sparrow hawk, woodpeckers, fieldfare and goldfinch.

STANHOPE

Stanhope, the capital of Upper Weardale, is a small town of great character and individuality, which marks the boundary between the softer scenery of lower Weardale and the wilder scenery to the west. The stone cross in the market place is the only reminder of a weekly market held in the town by virtue of a 1421 charter. The market continued until Victorian times, but today the town continues to serve the surrounding villages as an important local centre for shops and supplies.

Enjoying an attractive rural setting in the centre of the Dale, with a choice of local walks, Stanhope, in its quiet way, is becoming a small tourist centre with pleasant shops and cafés. Stanhope enjoyed its greatest period of prosperity in the 18th and 19th centuries when the lead and iron-stone industries were at their height, as reflected in the town's buildings and architecture.

The most dominant building in the Market Square is **Stanhope Castle**, a rambling structure complete with mock-Gothic crenellated towers, galleries and battlements. The building is, in fact, an elaborate folly built by the MP for Gateshead, Cuthbert Rippon in 1798 on the site of a medieval manor house. In 1875 it was enlarged to contain a private collection of mineral displays and stuffed birds for the entertainment of Victorian grouse-shooting parties. In the gardens is the

45 THE BAKER'S LOAF & WEARDALE TEA ROOMS

Stanhope, Bishop Auckland
A good variety of savoury and sweet delights are served in a popular bakery and tea room

see page 110

Fossil Tree Stump, Stanhope

46 ARDINE HOLIDAY COTTAGES

Wolsingham

Two cosy, traditional two-bedroom cottages well equipped for a self-catering break.

⊨ see page 110

Durham Dales Centre, which contains the Tourist Information centre, a tea room and a sculptured children's animal trail. The Dales Garden was first developed as an exhibit at the Gateshead National Gardens Festival in 1990 and has been re-created here using typical Dales cottage garden plants.

St Thomas's Church, by the Market Square, has a tower whose base is Norman, and some medieval glass in the west window. In the churchyard is a remarkable fossil tree stump which was discovered in 1962 in a local quarry.

The **Weardale Railway** runs for five miles between Stanhope and Wolsingham in the North Pennines Area of Outstanding Natural Beauty. Subject to availability, the trains are steam-hauled. Call 01845 600 1348 for timetable details.

Stanhope Old Hall, above Stanhope Burn Bridge, is generally accepted to be one of the most impressive buildings in Weardale. This huge, fortified manor house was designed to repel Scottish raiders. The privately owned hall itself is part medieval, part Elizabethan and part Jacobean. The outbuildings included a cornmill, a brew house and cattle yards.

One of the most important Bronze Age archaeological finds ever made in Britain was at Heathery Burn, a side valley off Stanhope Burn. In 1850, quarrymen cut through the floor of a cave to find a huge hoard of bronze and gold ornaments, amber necklaces, pottery, spearheads, animal bones and parts of chariots. The treasures are now kept in London's British Museum.

AROUND STANHOPE

FROSTERLEY

3 miles E of Stanhope on the A689

The village is famous for Frosterley marble, a black, heavily fossilised limestone that in former times was used extensively for rich decorative work and ornamentation on great public and private buildings throughout the north. The Chapel of the Nine Altars in Durham Cathedral makes extensive use of Frosterley Stone, sometimes called Durham Marble.

WOLSINGHAM

5 miles E of Stanhope on the A689

Wolsingham is one of the oldest market towns in County Durham and has its origins in Saxon times. The town has strong links with the iron and steel industries; Charles Attwood who was one of the great pioneers in the manufacture of steel founded the town steelworks, which once cast a variety of anchors and propellers for ships.

Tunstall Reservoir, north of Wolsingham, and reached by a narrow lane, lies in a valley of ancient oak woods alongside Waskerley Beck. The reservoir was built in the mid 19th century, originally to provide lime-free water for the locomotives of the Stockton and Darlington Railway to prevent their boilers from scaling like a domestic kettle. It now forms part of a delightful area to stroll, picnic or go fishing.

BLANCHLAND

7 miles N of Stanhope on the B6306

A small, serene estate village on the Northumberland and Durham border. This is another of the area's hidden places, and one well worth seeking out. The name Blanchland (white land) comes from the white habits worn by the canons of the Premonstratensian Order who founded Blanchland Abbey in 1665. The abbey was dissolved by Henry VIII in 1537. In 1702, Lord Crewe, the Bishop of Durham bought the Blanchland estate. On his death in 1721 the estates were left to the Lord Crewe Trustees who were responsible for building the picturesque village of Blanchland which you see today, using stone from the ruined Abbey buildings. Small cottages snuggle round a village square opposite the popular Lord Crewe Arms, housed in part of the priory next to the ancient abbey church of St Mary the Virgin.

POW HILL COUNTRY PARK

7 miles N of Stanhope on the B6306

Set in moorland overlooking the Derwent Reservoir, Pow Hill lies on the south shore and has great views of the lake. Conserved for its special wildlife interest, this valley bog habitat is home to goldcrests, coal tits, roe deer and red squirrels. The western end of the lake is protected as a nature reserve. In winter large flocks of migrant waders and wildfowl gather here.

Blanchland Priory

ROOKHOPE

3 miles NW of Stanhope off the A689

Rookhope (pronounced Rook-up), in lonely Rookhope Dale, is on the C2C cycle route, and has a history lost in antiquity, dating back to Roman times.

Another old fashioned Dale village, Rookhope is set in a hidden North Pennine valley. The remains of lead and iron mine activity now blend into quiet rural beauty. At one point the road climbs past Rookhope Chimney, part of a lead-smelting mill where poisonous and metallic-rich fumes were refined in long flues.

ALLENHEADS

9 miles NW of Stanhope on the B6295

Allenheads also has lead-mining connections, with its scatter of stone miners' cottages and an irregular village square with pub and chapel in a lovely setting. The village is a centre for fine, upland rambles through the surrounding hills, which still retain many signs

66   GO FISHING WITH NORTHUMBRIAN WATER

Derwent Reservoir

The lakes and reservoirs are set in some of the region's most spectacular countryside helping to make a visit to one of the waters a great day out for all the family.

 see page 122

of the former industrial activity. From Allenheads the main road climbs over Burtree Fell into Weardale, with wild moorland roads branching across to Rookhope to the east and Nenthead to the west.

WESTGATE AND EASTGATE

4 miles W of Stanhope on the A689

The area between the lovely stone built villages of Westgate and Eastgate was once the Bishop of Durham's deer park, kept to provide him with an abundant supply of venison. The villages are so called because they were the east and west 'gates' to the park. The foundations of the Bishop's castle can still be seen at Westgate along with an old mill and water wheel. In 1327 the troops of Edward III camped at Eastgate en route to Scotland to face the Scottish army.

ST JOHN'S CHAPEL

7 miles W of Stanhope on the A689

St John's Chapel is named after its parish church, dedicated to St John the Baptist. Like many of the surrounding villages, it was once a lead mining centre and is still the home of an annual Pennine sheep auction in September that attracts farmers from all over the North Pennines. This is the only village in Durham to boast a town hall, a small building dating from 1868 overlooking the village green.

The road from St John's Chapel to Langdon Beck in Teesdale rises to 2,056 feet as it passes over Harthope Fell, making it the highest classified road in England.

COWSHILL

8 miles W of Stanhope on the A689

In a hollow between Cowshill and Nenthead lies Killhope Mine. The Pennines have been worked for their mineral riches, lead in particular, since Roman times but until the 18th century the industry remained relatively primitive and small scale.

Mechanisation in the late 18th and early 19th century allowed the mining industry to grow until it was second only to coal as a major extractive industry in the region. Now the country's best-preserved lead-

Upper Weardale

mining site, Killhope Mine is the focal point of what is now the **North of England Lead Mining Museum**, dominated by the massive 34-feet water wheel. It used moorland streams, feeding a small reservoir, to provide power for the lead ore crushing mills, where the lead ore from the hillside mines was washed and crushed ready for smelting into pigs of lead. Much of the machinery in the Museum has been carefully restored by Durham County Council over recent years, together with part of the smelting mill, workshops, a smithy, tools and miners' sleeping quarters.

Weardale Museum, Ireshopeburn

IRESHOPEBURN

8 miles W of Stanhope on the A689

At Ireshopeburn, between Cowshill and St John's Chapel, is the delightful little **Weardale Museum & High House Chapel** situated in the former minister's house next to an 18th century Methodist chapel. The exhibits include a carefully re-created room in a typical Weardale lead-miners' cottage kitchen, with period furnishings and costumes, local history and mineral displays, and a room dedicated to John Wesley, who visited the area on several occasions. The museum is open during summer months only.

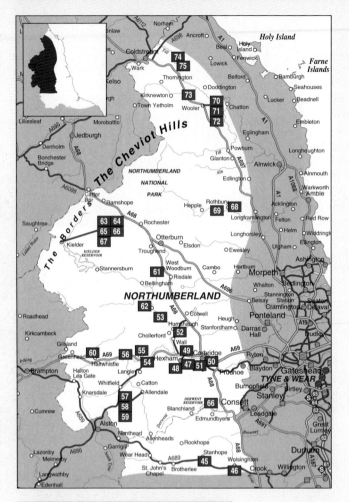

Hadrian's Wall & the Northumbrian National Park

West Northumberland, where the North Pennines blend into the Cheviots, is an exhilarating mixture of bleak grandeur, beauty and history. Stretching north towards the Scottish border are the 398 square miles of the Northumbrian National Park and the Kielder Forest Park, while to the south is Hadrian's Wall, that monumental feat of Roman civil engineering built on the orders of Emperor Hadrian in AD 122. A 73-mile-long World heritage Site, the wall marked the northern limit of the Roman Empire. Almost 2,000 years later it is still one of the world's most famous landmarks, stretching across mile after mile of glorious countryside.

Towards the east of the area, the hills slope down towards a stretch of fertile land with little towns like Rothbury and Wooler, which in themselves deserve exploration. But up on the high ground a person could walk for miles without meeting another soul. The highest point, at 2,650 feet, is the Cheviot itself, a few miles from the Scottish border.

This is the land of the Border Reivers, or mosstroopers, bands of marauding men from both sides of the Border who rustled, pillaged and fought among themselves, incurring the wrath of both the English and Scottish kings. A testament to their activities is the fact they gave the word blackmail to the English language. The 'mail' part of blackmail is an old Scottish word for a tax payment, and blackmail was a payment made by Border farmers to the Reivers as protection money. The Pennine Way passes over the moorland here, dipping occasionally into surprisingly green and wooded valleys. There are also less strenuous walks, circular routes and cycle tracks laid out, with maps and leaflets

PLACES OF INTEREST

available from the park visitor centres, at Rothbury, the quaintly-named Once Brewed, and Ingram. Here you can also learn about the history of the area as well as things to see.

Three main valleys penetrate the park from the east - Harthope Valley, Breamish Valley and Coquetdale. Harthope Valley is accessed from Wooler, along the Harthope Burn. Part of it is called Happy Valley, and is a popular beauty spot. There are a number of circular walks from the valley floor up into the hills and back again.

Breamish Valley is the most popular of the valleys, and it's here that the Ingram Visitors Centre, open in the summer months only, is located. Again, there are trails and walkways laid out.

Coquetdale is the gentlest of the three, and is popular with anglers. It winds up past Harbottle towards Alwinton and Barrowburn, but in so doing passes through the Otterburn Training Area, where up to 30,000 soldiers a year come to practise their artillery skills. This has actually preserved the upper part of Coquetdale from modern development, and farming here has changed little over the years. The valley is rich in wildlife, and heron, sandpiper and grey wagtail are common. The exposed crags support

Cawfields, nr Milecastle

rock-rose and thyme, and there are patches of ancient woodland.

The Kielder Forest covers 200 square miles, and is situated to the west of the National Park. It contains Europe's largest man-made lake, Kielder Water, opened by the Queen in 1982.

In the south of the National Park is by far the greater part of Hadrian's Wall, the best known Roman monument in Britain, and the best known Roman frontier in Europe. It stretches for 80 Roman miles (73 modern miles) across the country from Bowness-on-Solway in the west to Wallsend in the east, and in 1987 was declared a UNESCO World Heritage Site. A new national trail, the Hadrian's Wall Path runs for 84 miles following the rolling, northern terrain along the entire length of the Wall, and from May to September, the Hadrian's Wall Bus Service runs from Carlisle to Hexham (and Newcastle and Gateshead Metro Centre on a Sunday), stopping at the main attractions along the route. To see the Wall twisting across the moorland is an awe-inspiring site, and no visitor to Northumberland should miss it.

Cheviot Hills at Catcleugh Reservoir, nr Ramshope

HEXHAM

The picturesque market town of Hexham sits in the heart of Tynedale, and is its capital and administrative centre. It's rich in history and character and an ideal base from which to explore the Tyne Valley and Hadrian's Wall.

Hexham Abbey, one of the most important churches in the north of England, was at one time known as 'the largest and most magnificent church this side of the Alps'. It was founded by St Wilfrid in AD 674 after Queen Etheldreda of Northumbria granted him some land. The crypt of this early church remains almost intact, and access to it is via a stairway from the nave. The crypt was built using Roman stones, and on some of them you can still see inscriptions and carvings. Frith Stool, also known as St Wilfrid's chair, is a 1,300-year-old stone chair that is believed to have been used as a coronation throne for the ancient kings of Northumbria.

In 1130 a group of Augustinian canons set up an abbey on the site. The present church dates from the 13th century and contains some wonderful late-medieval architecture, which later restoration has not diminished. It has a rich heritage of carved stonework, and the early 16th century rood screen has been described as the best in any monastic church in Britain.

The Abbey was ransacked many times by the Scots armies, who at one time poured over the border into England. However, this

Hexham Abbey

was a two-way traffic, and the English did likewise to the abbeys at Melrose and Kelso.

The Abbey overlooks the Market Place, where a lively and colourful market is held each Tuesday. Nearby is the early 14th century Moot Hall, built of Roman stone. In olden days it served as the courtroom of the Archbishop of York, who held the grand title of Lord of the Liberty and Regality of Hexham. Today the hall houses the **Border History Library**, which contains material on Border life, in particular the music and poetry of the region.

Nearby, the Manor Office was England's first purpose-built prison and was built by the Archbishop in 1332 as a gaol for his courthouse. The Border History Museum is located within the gaol and tells, in a vivid way, the story of the border struggles between Scotland and England. For centuries the borderlands were virtually without

47 BOUCHON BISTROT

Hexham

Offering a touch of elegance, sophistication and relaxation in the French bistro style, the Bouchon Bistro is not to be missed.

see page 111

48 LOUGHBROW HOUSE

Hexham

Superior B&B accommodation in a distinguished 18th century manor house in a lovely garden setting high above the Tyne.

see page 112

49 THE RAT INN

Hexham

The Rat Inn is an award-winning restaurant with none of the stiffness, a true gem.

see page 111

rule of law, ravaged by bands of men known as Reivers - cattle rustlers and thieves who took advantage of the disputed border lands. Powerful wardens, or Lords of the Marches, themselves warlords of pitiless ferocity, were given almost complete authority by the king to control the Reivers and anyone else who crossed their path. However, for all their power and ferocity they were singularly unsuccessful in controlling the bloodshed. This was the period of the great border ballads, violent and colourful tales of love, death, heroism and betrayal, which have found an enduring place in literature.

The award-winning **Queens Hall Arts Centre** with theatre, café, library and exhibitions presents a full and varied programme throughout the year.

The town of Hexham has retained much of its character, with winding lanes and passageways, attractive 18th and 19th century houses, handsome terraces and some delightful shops and a market. There are some fine gardens around the abbey, and several attractive areas of open space. Tyne Green Country Park features attractive walks along the riverside and a picnic and barbecue site.

Hexham National Hunt Racecourse at Acomb is one of the most picturesque courses in the country. Call 01434 606881 for details of meetings. At Simonburn, just north of Hadrian's Wall, **St Mungo's Church** is the Mother Church of the North Tyne Valley.

AROUND HEXHAM

SLALEY

4 miles SE of Hexham, off the B6306

Slaley is a quiet village consisting of one long street with some picturesque houses dating from the 17th, 18th and 19th centuries. One of the finest houses - Church View

Queens Hall Arts Centre, Hexham

- stands opposite the 19th century St Mary's Church. Two miles southwest, Slayley Hall has some interesting gardens.

CORBRIDGE

3 miles E of Hexham on the A69

The lively market town of Corbridge was, for a time, the capital of the ancient Kingdom of Northumbria. The original Roman town, **Corstorpitum**, lay half a mile to the northwest, and was an important military headquarters. Visitors to the site can see the substantial remains of this strategic river crossing, which include a fine example of military granaries and two fortified medieval towers, which are evidence of more troubled times. The museum houses finds from the excavation of the site, the most famous of which is the Lion of Corbridge – a stone fountainhead. The 14th century Vicar's Pele was, as the name implies, formerly the home of the vicar, and the other, Low Hall, dating from the 13th century, was converted into a private house in 1675.

The finest building in Corbridge is undoubtedly **St Andrew's Church**. It still retains many Saxon features, and the base of the tower was once the west porch of the Saxon nave. Within the tower wall is a complete Roman arch, no doubt removed from Corstorpitum at some time. Corbridge is also the site of the **Northumberland County Show**, held each year on the late May Bank Holiday Monday.

AYDON

4 miles E of Hexham off the B6321

Aydon Castle is a superb example of a fortified manor house, such protection being necessary in this region in times past to keep the Reivers at bay. Built by Robert de Reymes in the late 13th century, it remains remarkably intact, and is often described as one of the best preserved fortified manor houses in Britain, thanks to its early owners and now to English Heritage.

CHOLLERFORD

5 miles N of Hexham on the B6318

The Roman fort of **Chesters**, or Cilurnum, to give it its Roman name, is situated in the parkland created by Nathaniel Clayton around the mansion he had built in 1771. The fort covers nearly six acres and was large enough to accommodate a full cavalry regiment. The **Museum** houses a remarkable collection of Roman antiquities. Remains of the Roman fort include a well preserved bath house and barracks. Near the bath house can be seen the foundations of a Roman bridge that carried a road across the Tyne.

Five minutes' walk from the Roman Fort is **Chesters Walled Garden**, laid out as a unique, organically run herb and herbaceous garden, with the original box hedges and cruciform layout giving it a timeless quality enhanced by the informal planting. The gardens house the national collections of thyme and marjoram, and other attractions include the

50 THE DYVELS INN

Corbridge

A fine old inn with a great atmosphere, hearty food and three en suite bedrooms.

see page 114

51 THE HAYES GUEST HOUSE

Corbridge

A choice of B&B and self-catering accommodation in an attractive setting close to the centre of Corbridge.

see page 113

66 GO FISHING WITH NORTHUMBRIAN WATER

Whittle Dene Lakes

The lakes and reservoirs are set in some of the region's most spectacular countryside helping to make a visit to one of the waters a great day out for all the family.

see page 122

52 GREENCARTS

Neal, Humshaugh, Hexham

A choice of B&B, bunkhouse and camping site on a farm next to Hadrian's Wall.

see page 114

53 HALLBARNS B&B

Hallbarns, Simonburn, nr Hexham

A traditional stone farmhouse in a beautiful setting close to Hadrian's Wall. Open all year for B&B guests.

see page 114

54 READING ROOMS

Haydon Bridge

This B & B is right by Haydon Bridge and the Tyne River and is an excellent base for sightseeing the North of England.

see page 115

Roman Garden and the giant Tibetan rhubarb. Many of the garden's 900 herbs are sold in the adjoining nursery. Open daily Easter to the end of October, otherwise by appointment. Tel: 01434 681483.

CHOLLERTON

5 miles N of Hexham on the A6079

Chollerton, six miles north of Hexham, enjoys an exceptionally fine setting. Nearby is the site of the Battle of Heavenfield, where King (later St) Oswald defeated the army of Cadwalla, a Welsh king.

BARRASFORD

7 miles N of Hexham off the A6079

Barrasford sits on the North Tyne across from **Haughton Castle**, of which there are fine views. The castle is one of the finest great houses in Northumberland, and dates originally from the 13th century. Over the succeeding years, additions and alterations have been made, with the west wing being designed by Anthony Salvin and

built in 1876. The castle isn't open to the public.

HAYDON BRIDGE

6 miles W of Hexham on the A69

Two bridges cross the Tyne here - a modern concrete one dating from 1970, and an older one dating from 1776. North of the village is Haydon Old Church, close to where the medieval village of Haydon lay. It dates partly from the 12th century.

LANGLEY

6 miles W of Hexham on the B6295

Langley Castle, now a hotel and restaurant, was built in around 1350. In 1450, Henry 1V had it destroyed, but it was restored in the 1890s by a local historian, Cadwallader Bates. In the 17th and early 18th centuries the Castle was owned by the Earls of Derwentwater, and in 1716 the third earl, James, was beheaded in London for his part in the 1715 Jacobite rebellion. His brother Charles was later beheaded for his

Haydon Bridge

Hadrian's Wall

part in the 1745 uprising. A memorial to them sits beside the A686 not far from the castle. Guided tours of the Castle and grounds are available by prior arrangement – Tel: 01434 688888.

Garden Station at Langley is an attractive, restored Victorian railway station in a woodland garden. A tranquil place with gardening and art courses, unusual plants and refreshments. Tel: 01434 684 391.

BARDON MILL
10 miles W of Hexham on the A69

Bardon Mill, a former mining village, stands on the north bank of the South Tyne. An important drovers' road crossed the river here and cattle were fitted with iron shoes at Bardon Mill to help them on their way to southern markets. The village is a convenient starting point for walks along **Hadrian's Wall** and the Roman forts of **Vindolanda** and **Housesteads** are nearby. At Vindolanda excavations continue to reveal fascinating insights into Roman life. An open air

museum features a reconstructed temple, shop and house. Perched high on a ridge, with splendid views of the surrounding countryside, the remains of Housesteads Fort cover over five acres and is one of the finest sections of Hadrians Wall. Nearby, **Once Brewed** is the main Visitor Centre for Hadrians Wall and the Northumberland National Park.

Between Bardon Mill and Haydon Bridge lies the confluence of the South Tyne and the River Allen, which, like the Tyne, comes from two main tributaries - the East Allen and West Allen. The valleys of the East and West Allen really are hidden jewels. The 22,667 acres of Allen Banks, as the lower part of the valley near the Tyne is known, is a deep, wooded, limestone valley, rich in natural beauty, now owned by the National Trust.

ALLENDALE
10 miles SW of Hexham on the B6295

Allendale Town lies on the River East Allen, set against a backdrop of heather clad moorland, and was

---

55 GRINDON CARTSHED

Hexham

Cosy B&B (self catering low season), perfect hosts and its surroundings have a wealth of experiences to offer the visitor. An absolute gem!

see page 115

56 VINDOLANDA AND ROMAN ARMY MUSEUM

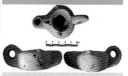

Hexham

Vindolanda, once a Roman frontier military and civilian site displays rare and fascinating objects from the past. Also worth a visit is the Roman Army Museum which gives an insight into life as a Roman soldier.

see page 116

57 THE GOLDEN LION

Allendale

A fine old traditional hosterly. You will find home-cooked food with old favourites such as Steak & Ale Pie. Well worth a visit.

see page 116

58 THE ALLENDALE INN

Allendale

A friendly, relaxed place where locals and visitors get together to enjoy a drink and a value-for-money snack or meal.

see page 117

59 ALLENDALE TEA ROOMS

Allendale

Popular tea rooms with a friendly, relaxed atmosphere and a varied daytime menu of value-for-money home cooking. Also two rooms for B&B.

see page 117

60 PILLAR BOX CAFÉ

Haltwhistle

Situated next to the Post Office of Haltwhistle, the Pillar Box Café provides a friendly and homely atmosphere for a relaxing dining experience.

see page 118

once an important centre of the north Pennine lead-mining industry. It retains attractive houses from prosperous times and a surprisingly large number of existing or former inns around the Market Square. A sundial in the churchyard in Allendale records the fact that the village lies exactly at the mid point between Beachy Head in Sussex and Cape Wrath in Scotland, making it the very centre of Britain.

HALTWHISTLE

15 miles W of Hexham on the A69

The origins of the name Haltwhistle are unknown but two suggestions are the watch (wessel) on the high (alt) mound, or the high (haut) fork of two streams (twysell). It is difficult to imagine that this pleasant little town with its grey terraces was once a mining area, but evidence of the local industries remain. An old pele tower is incorporated into the Centre of Britain Hotel in the town centre. Holy Cross Church, behind the Market Place, dates back to the 13th century and is said to be on the site of an earlier church founded by William the Lion, King of Scotland in 1178, when this area formed part of Scotland.

Three miles northwest of Haltwhistle, off the B6318, is **Walltown Quarry**, a recreation site built on the site of an old quarry. Today part of the Northumberland National Park, it contains laid-out trails and it is possible to spot oystercatchers, curlews, sandpipers and lapwings.

OTTERBURN

The village of Otterburn stands close to the centre of the National Park, in the broad valley of the River Rede. It makes an ideal base for exploring the surrounding countryside, an exhilarating area of open moorland and rounded hills. It was close to here, on a site marked by the 18th century Percy Cross, that the **Battle of Otterburn** took place in 1388 between the English and the Scots. By all accounts it was a ferocious encounter, even by the standards of the day, and one commentator said that it "was one of the sorest and best fought, without cowards or faint hearts".

Under the command of Earl Douglas, a gathering of Scottish troops at Jedburgh in 1388 had resolved to enter England in a two-pronged attack - one towards Carlisle and one down into Redesdale. In charge of the Redesdale contingent was the Earl of Douglas, who got as far as Durham before being forced back to the border by Henry Percy, better known as Hotspur, and his brother Ralph.

In August the English caught up with the Scottish army at Otterburn, and went straight into attack. The battle continued for many hours, gradually descending into a series of hand to hand fights between individual soldiers. Gradually the Scots got the upper hand, and captured both Percys. But it was a hollow victory, as the Earl of Douglas was killed. A second force under the Bishop of Durham hurried north when it heard the news, but it wisely decided not to engage in battle. A series of markers known as Golden Pots are said to mark the journey of Douglas's body when it was taken back to Melrose.

There are some interesting walks around Otterburn, and some well preserved remains of Iron Age forts can be seen on both Fawdon Hill and Camp Hill.

North of the village are the remains of **Bremenium** Roman fort. It was first built by Julius Agricola in the 1st century, though what the visitor sees now is mainly 3rd century. In its day the fort could hold up to 1,000 men, and was one of the defences along the Roman road now known as Dere Street. Close by is the **Brigantium Archaeological Reconstruction Centre**, where you can see a stone circle of 4000 BC, Iron Age defences, cup and ring carvings and a section of Roman road.

AROUND OTTERBURN

BELLINGHAM AND WARK
7 miles SW of Otterburn on the B6320

The North Tyne is fed by the Kielder Water, which on its way down to join the South Tyne above Hexham passes by the interesting villages of Bellingham and Wark.

Bellingham (pronounced Bellin-jam) is a small market town in a moorland setting, with a broad main street, market place and the austere little **St Cuthbert's**

Church, reflecting the constant troubles of the area in medieval times. To prevent marauding Scots from burning it down, a massive stone roof was added in the early 17th century.

In the churchyard an oddly shaped tombstone, somewhat reminiscent of a peddler's pack, is associated with a foiled robbery attempt that took place in 1723. A peddler arrived at Lee Hall, a mansion once situated between Bellingham and Wark, and asked if he could be put up for the night. As her master was away at the time the maid refused, but said that he could leave his heavy pack at the Hall and collect it the next day.

Imagine her consternation when some time later the pack began to move. Hearing her screams for help, a servant rushed to the scene and fired his gun at the moving bundle. When blood poured out and the body of an armed man was discovered inside, the servants realised that this had been a clever attempt to burgle the Hall. They sounded a horn, which they found inside the pack next to the body, and when the robber's accomplices came running in response to the prearranged signal, they were speedily dealt with.

Wark, to the south of Bellingham, is an attractive estate village, once part of the lordship of Wark. The Scottish kings are said to have held court here in the 12th century. **Chipchase Castle**, is a combination of 14th century tower, Jacobean mansion and Georgian interior. A walled nursery garden is

Otterburn Mill dates from the 18th century, though a mill is thought to have stood on the site from at least the 15th century. Production of woollens ceased in 1976, but the mill is still open and on display are Europe's only original working tenterhooks, where newly woven cloth was stretched and dried

61 THE BAY HORSE INN

West Woodburn, Kielder
A mellow sandstone hostelry where drinkers, diners and overnight guests are all made equally welcome.

🍴 🛏 see page 118

62 CHIPCHASE CASTLE

Wark-on-Tyne
Medieval/Jacobean castle with 3 stunning acres of gardens, open to the public.

🏛 see page 119

63 TWENTY SEVEN B&B

Kielder

A quiet, comfortable spot for discovering the stunning scenery, dark skies, the wildlife and the outdoor facilities of Kielder Water & Forest Park.

 see page 119

64 KIELDER WATER & FOREST PARK

Kielder

Home to Northern Europe's largest man-made lake, England's largest forest and officially the country's most tranquil spot, Kielder Water & Forest Park is not to be missed.

 see page 120

65 LEAPLISH WATERSIDE PARK

Kielder

Leaplish Waterside Park boasts luxury self catering forest lodges, an indoor heated swimming pool and sauna, restaurant and bar and the Kielder Birds of Prey centre.

  see page 121

open to the public throughout the summer months but the castle itself is only open on June afternoons. Tel: 01434 230203

On the slopes overlooking the North Tyne are a large number of unusually named prehistoric settlements, such as Male Knock Camp, Good Wife Camp, Nigh Folds Camp, Carryhouse Camp and Shieldence Camp.

KIELDER

16 miles W of Otterburn off the B6320

Kielder village was built in the 1950s to house workers employed in the man-made **Kielder Forest**, which covers 200 square miles to the west of the **Northumberland National Park**.

Here at Kielder Forest you'll find one of the few areas in Britain that is home to more red squirrels than grey, thanks to careful forest planning that ensures a constant supply of conifer preferred by red squirrels. Otters, too, are resident in Kielder, and the area abounds with deer and rare birds and plants.

There's some excellent walking to be had, with several marked trails and routes to suit all abilities, from a leisurely stroll to an energetic climb, with maps and leaflets to guide you round. There are also cycle routes, including the 17 mile Kielder Water Cycle Route, and bicycles can be hired from the local visitors centre.

Within the forest is **Kielder Water**, opened by the Queen in 1982; it is the largest man-made lake in Northern Europe with over 27 miles of shoreline. The visitor

Kielder Water

can take a pleasure cruise aboard the Osprey, an 80-seat passenger cruiser that stops at several points of interest along the lake.

Located at sites around the lake and within the forest is an art and sculpture trail of works inspired by the surroundings. **Leaplish Waterside Park** has a range of activities and attractions for all ages, including one of the largest and most fascinating collections of birds of prey in the North of England. Tel: 01434 250400

To the northwest is **Kielder Castle**, at one time a hunting lodge for the Duke of Northumberland, and later offices for the Forestry Commission. It is now a fascinating visitor centre with exhibits describing the development of the forest and the birdlife that is found in Kielder.

ELSDON

3 miles E of Otterburn on the B6341

The village of Elsdon is of great historical importance. Built around a wide green, with **St Cuthbert's Church** in the middle, it was the medieval capital of Redesdale - the most lawless place in Northumberland, and scene of some of the worst border fighting. In later years it became an important stopping point on the drovers' road.

In the late 19th century, when the church was being restored, over 1,000 skulls were uncovered. They are thought to be those of soldiers killed at the Battle of Otterburn.

Elsdon Tower, which in 1415 was referred to as the 'vicar's pele',

Elsdon Tower

dates from the 14th century, though it was largely rebuilt at a later date. It is one of the most important pele towers of the region and is now a private residence.

ROTHBURY

12 miles E of Otterburn on the B6341

The attractive town of Rothbury is a natural focal point from which to explore the valley of the River Coquet. It is an excellent starting point for some delightful walks, either along the valley or through the nearby woodland. The most famous perhaps being the trail to the Rothbury Terraces, a series of parallel tracks along the hillside above the town.

Simonside, a hill offering a fine viewpoint, is steeped in history and the subject of several legends. Flint arrowheads have been recovered there, as well as bronze swords, shards of pottery, axe heads and ornaments. Burial cairns abound, as do carved stones and ancient paths. The Northumberland

---

66 GO FISHING WITH NORTHUMBRIAN WATER

Kielder Water and Forest Park

The lakes and reservoirs are set in some of the region's most spectacular countryside helping to make a visit to one of the waters a great day out for all the family.

 see page 122

67 KIELDER WATER BIRDS OF PREY CENTRE

Kielder

The centre contains one of the largest and most fascinating collections of Birds of prey in the north of England.

 see page 123

68 THE ELM TREE COFFEE SHOP

Rothbury

A friendly, family-run coffee shop open every day for a selection of excellent, value-for-money snacks and meals.

see page 124

69 THE THREE WHEAT HEADS

Thropton

A delightful hostelry in a picturesque setting, with great food and drink and superior B&B accommodation.

see page 125

National Park has prepared a leaflet, which guides you on a walk up and onto the hill.

To the north of Simonside is Lordenshaws, with a well defined hill fort, Bronze Age burial mounds, rock carvings and cairns.

From the 18th century the village of Rothbury developed into a natural marketplace for Upper Coquetdale, to which cattle and sheep were brought for sale, and the drovers were provided with numerous alehouses. Since the mid 19th century Rothbury has been a holiday resort for walkers and fishermen, and the railway, which opened in 1870, contributed further to its growth.

The former Saxon parish church of Rothbury, which was almost entirely rebuilt in 1850, is worth visiting to see the font, which stands on part of the 9th century Rothbury cross.

Just outside Rothbury is the house and estate of **Cragside**, once the home of Sir William Armstrong, arms manufacturer and industrialist.

He bought 14,000 acres in the valley of the Debden Burn, and employed architect Norman Shaw to extend the existing house and make it suitable to entertain royalty and other wealthy guests. Work began in 1864, and what finally emerged in 1884 was a mock-Tudor Victorian mansion. A pioneer of the turbine, Armstrong designed various pieces of apparatus for the house, and devised his own hydroelectric systems, with man-made lakes, streams and miles of underground piping, making Cragside the first house in the world to be lit by hydroelectricity. Cragside is now owned by the National Trust, and has been sympathetically restored to show how upper middle class Victorians were beginning to combine comfort, opulence and all the latest technology in their homes.

With one of Europe's largest rock gardens, 40 miles of walks and 7 million tress and shrubs, including England's tallest Douglas fir, Cragside is a garden of superlatives and great drama. The 1,000 acres include 8,000 heathers and a vast woodland garden famous for its rhododendron and azalea displays.

WELDON BRIDGE

15 miles E of Otterburn on the A697

Weldon Bridge is an exceptionally elegant bridge across the River Coquet, dating from 1744. Although it no longer carries the main road, it remains an impressive feature.

Nearby is **Brinkburn Priory**, standing in secluded woodland on the banks of the river. It was established in about 1135 by

Cragside, Rothbury

William de Bertram, 1st Baron Mitford, and is thought to have been built by the same masons who constructed nearby Longframlington church. It is in a beautiful setting surrounded by ancient trees and rhododendrons, and was once painted by Turner as a romantic ruin. Its church was restored in 1859 by Thomas Austin on behalf of the Cadogan family, and has many fine architectural features. It is also the setting for famous annual summer concerts.

LONGFRAMLINGTON

15 miles E of Otterburn on the A697

Longframlington derives its name from its principal family, the de Framlingtons, who are recorded as the 12th-century benefactors of Brinkburn Priory. The route of the Devil's Causeway, a Roman road between Hadrian's Wall and the Scottish border, can easily be traced west of the village, along what is now a farm lane past Framlington Villa.

There are few shops here but the village retains the traditional craftsmanship of a Northumbrian pipe maker. The workshop, where you can see the production of these unique and beautiful musical instruments, is open to the public.

HEPPLE

8 miles NE of Otterburn on the B6341

Hepple has a reminder of the difficulty of life near the borders in the form of **Hepple Tower**, a 14th century pele tower built so strongly that attempts to demolish it and use the stone for a new farmhouse had

to be abandoned. West of the village, on the moors, are some fine examples of fortified houses and farms.

WOOPERTON

20 miles NE of Otterburn off the A697

Wooperton is close to the site of the **Battle of Hedgeley Moor**, which took place in 1464. In truth this was more of a skirmish, in which the Yorkist Lord Montague defeated the Lancastrian Sir Ralph Percy, who was killed. The site of the Battle of Hedgeley Moor is marked by a carved stone called the Percy Cross and can be reached along a short footpath leading from the A697.

WOOLER

Wooler is a small town standing on the northern edge of the Cheviots, midway between Newcastle and Edinburgh, and is an excellent centre for exploring both the Cheviots and the border country. In the 18th and early 19th centuries it became an important halt on the

66 GO FISHING WITH NORTHUMBRIAN WATER

Fontburn Reservoir

The lakes and reservoirs are set in some of the region's most spectacular countryside helping to make a visit to one of the waters a great day out for all the family.

 see page 122

College Valley, nr Wooler

70 THE ANCHOR INN

Wooler

A warm, welcome, friendly chat, value-for-money home cooking and comfortable accommodation in the little town of Wooler.

see page 126

71 THE WHEATSHEAF HOTEL

Wooler

A friendly hostelry that combines the best features of a much-loved local eating and drinking place and a quiet, comfortable base for tourists.

see page 126

72 MOJO'S CAFÉ

Wooler

A very friendly, relaxed café/bistro on the main street, with an all-day selection of sweet and savoury snacks and meals.

see page 127

main north-south coaching route and now holds regular markets of sheep and cattle.

There are superb walking opportunities in the area surrounding Wooler, for example, the Iron Age hill fort immediately west of the town, Earle Whin and Wooler Common, or via Harthope onto The Cheviot itself. Alternatively, the visitor can take a vehicle into the Harthope Valley with a choice of walks, easy or strenuous, up and through the magnificent hillsides of this part of the Northumberland National Park.

The visitor can also climb **Humbledon Hill**, on top of which are the remains of a hill fort, built about 300 BC. The Battle of Humbledon Hill was fought here in 1402 between the English and the Scots, who had been on a raiding mission as far south as Newcastle. Due to the firepower of Welsh bowmen in the English army, the Scottish army assembled within the fort was easily defeated. Human and horse bones have been uncovered while Humbledon Hill's northern slopes were being ploughed, and an area is still known to this day as Red Riggs from the blood, which stained the ground during and after the battle.

AROUND WOOLER

KIRKNEWTON

6 miles W of Wooler on the B6351

Kirknewton is a typical border village made up of cottages, a school and village church. **St Gregory's Church** dates mainly

from the 19th century, though there are medieval fragments such as an unusual sculpture, which shows the Magi wearing kilts – a fascinating example of medieval artists presenting the Christian story in ways their audience could understand.

Josephine Butler, the great Victorian social reformer and fighter for women's rights, who retired to Northumberland and died here in 1906, is buried in the churchyard. Her father had been a wealthy landowner, and a cousin of British Prime Minister Earl Grey of Howick Hall, near Craster.

Half a mile east of Kirknewton, in what are now fields by the River Glen, lay the royal township of Gefrin or Ad-Gefrin, better known as Yeavering. Discovered in 1948 thanks to aerial photography, this was where, in the 7th century, King Edwin of Northumbria built a huge wooden palace that included a royal hall over 100 feet long, storehouses, stables, chapels and living quarters. A stone, and a board explaining the layout, now mark the place where this long-vanished royal establishment once stood.

BRANXTON

8 miles NW of Wooler off the A697

The site of the decisive **Battle of Flodden Field** can be found near Branxton, marked by a cross in a cornfield reached by a short path. Following the terms of a Scottish alliance with the French King James IV of Scotland led his 30,000 troops into England after Henry

VIII had invaded France. An English army of some 20,000 men under the Earl of Surrey marched north in response and in the ensuing battle the Scots were routed, with the loss of up to 10,000 men, and the king killed.

Etal Castle

The tragedy is commemorated in the lament *The Flowers of the Forest*, played by pipers at the Remembrance Sunday ceremony.

CORNHILL-ON-TWEED

10 miles NW of Wooler at the junction of the A697 and A698

An unusual attraction near Cornhill is **Heatherslaw Cornmill**, a 19th century cornmill restored to working order, producing stoneground wholemeal flour. It's open daily from mid-March to the end of September, and in winter Monday, Friday and other dates when milling. Tel: 01890 820338.

FORD AND ETAL

4 miles E of Cornhill-on-Tweed on the B6353 (Ford) or B6354 (Etal)

The twin estate villages of Ford and Etal were built in the late-19th century. Ford is a 'model' village with many beautiful stone buildings and well-tended gardens. Dating originally from the 14th century but heavily restored in the 19th, **Ford Castle** was the home of Louisa Ann, Marchioness of Waterford. In 1860 she built the village school and spent the next 20 or so years decorating it with murals depicting biblical scenes. As models she used local families, thus creating a pictorial gallery of life and work in the area at that time. Now known as **Lady Waterford Hall**, it is open daily in the summer for visits. Etal is an attractive village within which are the ruins of the 14th century castle destroyed by King James IV of Scotland. The **Church of the Blessed Virgin Mary** was built in 1858 by Lady Augusta Fitzclarence in memory of her husband and daughter.

73 THE RED LION INN

Milfield, nr Wooler

A cosy, welcoming inn with real ales, wholesome, good-value food and roomy B&B accommodation.

 see page 127

74 THE BLACK BULL

Etal Village, Cornhill-on-Tweed

A pretty thatched village pub that's the hub of the community, with home-cooked food, a good choice of drinks and a thriving social side. Self-catering accommodation in the same ownership near Rothbury.

see page 128

75 LADY WATERFORD HALL

Ford

Home of the Waterford Gallery. Commissioned in 1860 by Louisa Anne, Marchionness of Waterford.

see page 128

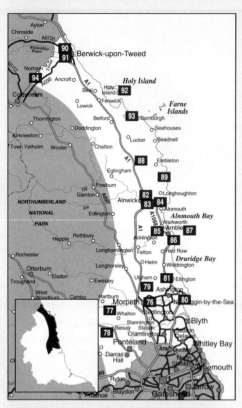

The Northumberland Coastal Area

Stretching from the edge of the Cheviots to the East Coast, and from the River Blyth in the south to Berwick-upon-Tweed in the north, this is an area of quiet villages and small market towns, majestic castles, and what many people consider to be the finest coastline in England. Designated as the North Northumberland Heritage Coast, the area boasts a wealth of historical attractions such as Bamburgh Castle, Lindisfarne and the Farne Islands.

For all its beauty, it's a quiet coastline, and you can walk for miles along the dunes and beaches without meeting another soul. No deck chairs or noisy ice cream vans here - just a quietness broken occasionally by the screeching of gulls. Coquet Island is a renowned bird sanctuary where the visitor can see puffins, roseate terns, razorbills, cormorants and eiders.

Lindisfarne, a small island lying between Bamburgh and Berwick, is perhaps the most evocative place of all on the coast. It was to here that St Aidan and a small community of Irish monks came from Iona in AD 635 to found a monastery from which missionaries set out to convert northern England to Christianity.

The region has withstood a tempestuous past and has been the focus of fierce fighting, nowhere more so than the Border town of Berwick, whose strategic location made it a prime target in the endless skirmishes between the English and the Scots. All along the coastline can be seen superb castles; some have been converted into grand mansions for the great families of the area, while others are now no more than ruins.

Inland from the coast the land is heavily farmed, and there is a pleasant landscape of fields, woodland, country lanes and farms. The villages, with their ancient parish churches and village greens, are especially fine. The village green was essential in olden times, as the Scots constantly harried this area, and the villagers needed somewhere to guard their cattle after bringing them in from the surrounding land.

The area to the southeast, around Ashington, was once coal mining country, though the scars are gradually being swept away. The industry is remembered in a museum of mining at Woodhorn. Even here however, an earlier history is evident, as the former Woodhorn church is one of the most interesting in Northumberland.

One of the North East's greatest sons - George Stephenson was born in Wylam, a village to the west of Newcastle. His story is told in the Stephenson Railway Museum, North Shields.

Alnwick Castle

71

MORPETH

The county town of Morpeth seems far removed, both in spirit and appearance, from the mining areas further down the Wansbeck valley. An attractive market town, Morpeth was once a stopping point on the A1 from Newcastle and Edinburgh, before the days of bypasses, and some fine inns were established to serve the former travellers.

The Norman's built a castle here that stood in what is now **Carlisle Park**. It was destroyed by William Rufus in 1095. A second castle was built close by, but was demolished by King John in 1215. It was subsequently rebuilt, but was mostly destroyed yet again by Montrose in 1644. Known as **Morpeth Castle**, it is now a restored gatehouse, managed by the Landmark Trust and is open once a year.

The third - which isn't really a castle but has the appearance of one - was built by John Dobson in 1828 as the county gaol and courthouse. Still standing, it is now private apartments and self catering accommodation.

The **Clock Tower** in the middle of Oldgate has been heightened several times. It probably dates from the early 17th century, though medieval stone was used in its construction. In its time it has served as a gaol and a place from where the nightly curfew was sounded. Its bells were a gift from a Major Main, who was elected MP for the town in 1707. He had intended them for Berwick, but they didn't elect him, so, as a local saying goes, "the bells of Berwick still ring at Morpeth". The Clock Tower is one of only a handful of such buildings in England. The Town Hall was built to designs by Vanbrugh, and a handsome bridge over the Wansbeck was designed by Telford.

Morpeth's St Mary's Church, lying to the south of the river, dates from the 14th century. It has some of the finest stained glass in Northumberland. In the churchyard is the grave of Suffragette Emily Davison, who was killed under the hooves of Anmer, the king's horse, during the 1913 Derby meeting. Her funeral attracted thousands of people to Morpeth. About a mile west of the town are the scant remains of Newminster Abbey, a Cistercian foundation dating from the 12th century. It was founded by monks from Fountains Abbey in Yorkshire.

Not to be missed is the 13th century **Morpeth Chantry** on Bridge Street, one of only five bridge chantries still in existence. Originally the Chapel of All Saints, it has been in its time a cholera hospital, a mineral water factory and a school where the famous Tudor botanist William Turner was educated. Nowadays it houses the **Chantry Bagpipe Museum**, a unique museum specialising in the history and development of Northumbrian small pipes and their music. The town's tourist information centre is also located here, as are a craft centre, a picture framers and a mountain sports shop.

There are two attractions for

animal-lovers in the area: the Sanctuary Wildlife Care Centre at Crowden Hill Farm, Ulgham (Tel: 01670 791778), and the Whitehouse Farm Centre with hundreds of animals to feed, hold or stroke (Tel: 01670 789988).

AROUND MORPETH

CAMBO
11 miles W of Morpeth off the B6342

The renowned landscape gardener Lancelot 'Capability' Brown was born here in 1716. **Wallington Hall**, lying deep in the heart of the Northumbrian countryside, is a National Trust property dating from 1688. The two great families associated with the place - the Blacketts and the Trevelyans - have each made their own mark on what must be one of the most elegant houses in Northumberland. In the Great Hall is a famous collection of paintings about Northumbrian history, and one of the rooms has an unusual collection of dolls' houses. The 18th century landscaped grounds (influenced by local man 'Capability' Brown, who went to school in the estate village) include lawns, shrubberies, lakes and woodland, ornamental buildings, sculptures and water features.

BELSAY
7 miles SW of Morpeth on the A696

Belsay Hall was built for Sir Charles Monck on an estate that already had a castle and a Jacobean mansion. Set in 30 acres of landscaped gardens, Belsay Hall is

Wallington Hall, Cambo

Greek in style and contains the architecturally splendid Great Hall. Two miles west is the Bolam Lake Country Park, with a 25 acre lake, trails and picnic areas

BEDLINGTON
5 miles SE of Morpeth off the A189

Bedlington, formerly known as the county town of Bedlingtonshire, was a district of the County Palatinate of Durham until 1844, when it was incorporated into Northumberland. The town became the centre of a prosperous mining and iron-founding community and has two important links with railway history. The rolled-iron rails for the Stockton and Darlington Railway were manufactured here, and it is also the birthplace of the great locomotive engineer, Sir Daniel Gooch. One of the greatest engineers of his day, Sir Daniel was the locomotive

78 BELSAY HALL CASTLE AND GARDENS

Belsay

The hall was built for Sir Charles Monck on an estate that already had a castle and Jacobean mansion, and they all stand in 30 beautiful acres of landscaped gardens.

 see page 128

79 MICKLEWOOD PARK

Longhirst, Morpeth

Top-quality self-catering holiday accommodation in units catering for between 4 and 10 guests. Lots of on-site sporting and leisure facilities.

 see page 130

80 NEVIN'S NIBBLES

Newbiggin-by-the-Sea

A bright, vibrant café/restaurant on the seafront, with a wide-ranging daylong menu of home-cooked snacks and meals.

 see page 131

81 HAGG FARMHOUSE B&B

Ellington, Morpeth

Comfortable farmhouse B&B accommodation close to many of the region's coastal and country attractions.

see page 131

superintendent on the Great Western Railway, and the man who first linked up North America and Europe via a telegraph line.

There is an attractive country park near Bedlington at Humford Mill, with an information centre and nature trails. At Plessey Woods, south west of the town, another country park extends along the wooded banks of the River Blyth, around Plessey Mill, with trails and a visitor centre.

ASHINGTON

5 miles E of Morpeth on the A197

Ashington is a sprawling town around the River Wansbeck, built to serve the mining industry. The two-mile-long **Wansbeck Riverside Park**, which has been developed along the embankment, offers sailing and angling facilities, plus a four mile walk along the mouth of the River Wansbeck. The famous footballing brothers Bobby and Jackie Charlton were born in Ashington in the 1930s, and the cricketer Stephen Harmison is also a son of the town. In the stunning Cutter building and original colliery structures **Woodhorn**, in the QEII Country Park, tells the story of coal mining and miners. Woodhorn is also home to Northumberland's archival treasures, with all kinds of records dating back 800 years. Tel: 01670 528080.

WOODHORN

6 miles E of Morpeth on the A197

At Woodhorn, close to Ashington, there is the fascinating late-Anglo-Saxon St Mary's Church, said to be

the oldest church building in Northumberland. The outside was heavily restored in 1843, though the inside is almost wholly pre-Norman. There is a 13th century effigy of Agnes de Velence, wife of Hugh de Baliol, brother of the Scottish king, John Baliol.

The Woodhorn Colliery Museum, which is linked to the Queen Elizabeth Country Park by a short light railway, offers interesting displays of mining life and the social history of the area. 'Turning the Pages' is an award winning, interactive exhibition on the Lindisfarne Gospels.

NEWBIGGIN BY THE SEA

7 miles E of Morpeth on the A197

Newbiggin by the Sea is a fishing village and small resort enjoying an attractive stretch of coastline with rocky inlets and sandy beaches, now much improved after the ravages of the coal industry. St Bartholomew's Church has a particularly interesting 13th century interior. The village has the oldest operational lifeboat house in Britain, built in 1851.

LONGHORSLEY

6 miles N of Morpeth off the A697

Longhorsley is noted for being the home of Thomas Bell, inventor of self-raising flour. He called it Bell's Royal, but the name was later changed to Bero.

Born at Blackheath in London in 1872, Emily Davison spent a lot of time in the village. A plaque on the wall of the post office, her former home, commemorates her death under the hooves of the King's horse at Epsom in 1913. Her suffragette activities are remembered by the local Women's Institute each year when flowers are placed on her grave in the family grave in Morpeth.

ALNWICK

Alnwick (pronounced Annick) is one of Northumberland's most impressive towns. It still retains the feel and appearance of a great medieval military and commercial centre, being an important market town since the granting of its charter in 1291. The town is dominated by the huge fortress of **Alnwick Castle**, set in beautiful parklands designed and landscaped in the 18th century by Capability Brown and Thomas Call. Alnwick Castle began, like most of Northumberland's castles, as a Norman motte and bailey. In the 12th century this was replaced by a stone castle, which was greatly added to over the centuries. In 1309, the castle came into the possession of Henry de Percy, who strengthened the fortifications. Henry's great grandson was made an earl, and the castle was then passed down 11 generations of Earls. When the male Percy line died out, it passed through the female line to Sir Hugh Smithson, who took the Percy name and was created Duke of Northumberland. When the Duke inherited the castle in 1750 it was falling into disrepair and he commissioned the renowned Robert Adam to restore

Alnwick Castle

the castle into a residence fit for a Duke. The superb ceilings and fireplaces can still be seen today. Further sweeping changes were made in the 1850s and 1860s, when the 4th Duke commissioned the Victorian architect Anthony Salvin to transform the castle into a great country house with all modern comforts while recapturing its former medieval glory. Visitors can admire the Italian Renaissance-style State Rooms and treasures that include paintings by Titian, Tintoretto, Canaletto and Van Dyck, collections of Meissen china and exquisite furniture.

There is also an impressive archaeological museum and extensive archive collections, as well as the Fusiliers of Northumberland Museum housed in The Abbot's Tower.

The castle is the home of the Percys to this day, and is a favourite location for making films, including Robin Hood Prince of Thieves and the Harry Potter films, where it doubles as Hogwart's School.

82   THE ALNWICK GARDEN

Alnwick

A garden which is a place of contemplation, a place of fun, a place of inspiration and education.

 see page 132

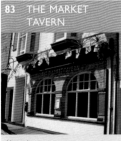

83 THE MARKET TAVERN

Alnwick

One of the most popular hostelries in the area – for a drink in the sociable bar, a meal or an overnight stay.

🍴 🛏 see page 133

•

Each year on Shrove Tuesday Alnwick is host to an annual tradition that begins with the Duke throwing a ball over the castle wall into the town and ends when the ball is retrieved from the river. Traditionally the head of a Scotsman was used, but today the game is played using a more conventional football.

•

84 THE COACH INN

Lesbury, Alnwick

A lovely old inn where visitors can look forward to a warm welcome and a meal to remember in good company and charming surroundings.

🍴 see page 134

The present Duke and Duchess of Northumberland are responsible for one of the most exciting contemporary gardens to be developed in recent years. The Duchess's vision was to create a beautiful public space open to everyone for contemplation, fun, inspiration and relaxation – and she has realized it on a grand scale. The impressive **Alnwick Garden** boasts a superb Grand Cascade – one of the finest water features in Europe, and other gardens include the Rose Garden, the Serpent garden, the Labyrinth, the ornamental Garden, the Poison Garden with ivy-covered tunnels, one of the world's largest treehouses and a new pavilion and visitor centre. There are 3 miles of box hedges, every inch of which are hand-clipped twice a year. Tel: 01665 511350

Hulne Park, landscaped by the great Northumbrian born 'Capability Brown', encompasses the ruins of Hulne Priory, the earliest Carmelite Foundation in England dating from 1242.

Alnwick town itself is worthy of a leisurely exploration among the evocatively named ancient narrow streets of Pottergate, Fenkle Street, Green Batt, Bondgate Without and Bondgate Within. A road leads through the narrow arch of Hotspur Tower, the one surviving part of the town's fortifications, built by the second Duke of Northumberland in the 15th century. All that's left of the once mighty Alnwick Abbey is its 15th century gatehouse, situated just beyond Canongate Bridge.

St Michael's Church in Alnwick overlooks the River Aln, and dates from the 15th century. It was unusual in a place as lawless as Northumberland at that time to build a church as large and as splendid as St Michael's.

The popular and colourful Alnwick Fair, dating from the 13th century, takes place each June.

Low Tide, Alnmouth

AROUND ALNWICK

ALNMOUTH

3 miles E of Alnwick off the A1068

Alnmouth is a small seaside resort at the mouth of the River Aln, with fine sandy beaches and two golf courses. The village dates back to the 8th century and was the main sea port for the town of Alnwick in the Middle Ages. John Paul Jones, the Scot who founded the American navy, bombarded the port during the American War of Independence.

The village of Alnmouth is the starting point for many excellent walks along superb stretches of coastline both southwards, past extensive dunes to Warkworth, and north to the former fishing village of Boulmer.

WARKWORTH

6 miles SE of Alnwick on the A1068

At the southern end of Alnmouth Bay, on the River Coquet, lies **Warkworth Castle**. The site has been fortified since the Iron Age, though the first stone castle was probably built by one 'Roger, son of Richard', who had been granted the castle by Henry II in the 12th century.

What can be seen now is mainly late 12th and 13th century, including the great Carrickfergus Tower and the West Postern Towers, built by Roger's son, Robert. The castle came into the ownership of the Percys in 1332 and the family lived here up until the 16th century. The family crest can be seen on the Lion Tower.

The most famous of all the

River Coquet, Warkworth

Percy's, Harry (known as Hotspur) was brought up here.

In 1399 the family created history for the role they played in placing Henry Bolingbroke on the throne as Henry IV. The castle is now in the care of English Heritage and is a delightful sight in spring when the grass mound on which it stands is covered with thousands of daffodils. Tel: 01665 711423

An unusual and interesting walk is signposted to The Hermitage, along the riverside footpath below the castle, where a ferry takes you across the river to visit the tiny chapel hewn out of solid rock. It dates from medieval times and was in use until late in the 16th century.

Warkworth is an interesting and beautiful village in its own right. An imposing fortified gatehouse on the 14th century bridge, now only used by pedestrians, would enable an invading army to be kept at bay north of the Coquet. **St Lawrence's Church** is almost entirely Norman, though its spire - an unusual feature

85 THE MASONS ARMS

Warkworth, nr Morpeth
A distinguished inn serving a good choice of drinks and classic pub dishes, with a nearby Grade II listed house for superior B&B accommodation.

see page 135

86 CEDAR CAFÉ

Amble, nr Morpeth

A popular daytime eating place near the harbour and beach, serving anything from cakes and sandwiches to full meals.

 see page 134

87 COQUET ISLAND

Amble

The island, with its unusual square-towered lighthouse, is owned by the Duke of Northumberland and managed by the RSPB as a nature reserve.

 see page 136

on medieval churches in Northumberland - dates from the 14th century.

AMBLE

7 miles SE of Alnwick on the A1068

Amble is a small port situated at the mouth of the River Coquet, once important for the export of coal, but now enjoying new prosperity as a marina and sea-fishing centre, with a carefully restored harbour. It is a lively place, particularly when the daily catches of fish are being unloaded.

A mile offshore lies **Coquet Island**. It was here that St Cuthbert landed in AD 684. The island's square-towered lighthouse was built in 1841 on the ruins of a 15th century monastery known as Cocwadae. Parts of the monastic building have survived, including a Benedictine cell dating from the 14th century.

Coquet Island had a reputation in former times for causing shipwrecks, but is now a celebrated bird sanctuary, noted for colonies

of terns, puffins and eider ducks. Managed by the Royal Society for the Protection of Birds, the island can be visited by boat trips departing from Amble quayside throughout the summer.

DRURIDGE BAY

12 miles SE of Alnwick off the A1068

Druridge Bay Country Park includes Ladyburn Lake, where there is sailing and windsurfing, plus walking trails, a visitor centre and picnic area. The whole area was once a huge opencast coalmine before it was landscaped and opened as a park in 1989. Nearby are the ruins of medieval Chibburn Preceptory - a small medieval house and chapel that belonged to the Knights Hospitaller.

EDLINGHAM

5 miles SW of Alnwick on the B6341

Edlingham mustn't be confused with the villages of Eglingham and Ellingham, both a few miles to the north. Here at Edlingham the moorland road crosses Corby's Crags, affording visitors one of the finest views in Northumberland. The panorama encompasses the Cheviot Hills in the north, whilst to the south a rolling landscape of heather moors and crags stretches as far as Hadrian's Wall. On a clear day it's possible to catch a glimpse of the high peaks of the North Pennines.

Edlingham Castle was built in the 12th century, but abandoned in 1650 when parts of it collapsed. The ruins were originally thought to be of a simple Northumbrian tower house, but excavations in the

Druridge Bay

late 1970s and early 1980s showed it as having been much more substantial than that.

EGLINGHAM

6 miles NW of Alnwick on the B6346

St Maurice's Church dates from about 1200, and was built on a site granted to the monks of Lindisfarne in AD 738 by King Ceowulf of Northumbria. In 1596 it was attacked by the Scots, and part of the chancel had to be rebuilt in the early 17th century.

A few bumps in a field not far away indicate where the village once stood, and a mile to the southwest is a small hill fort with the quaint name of The Ringses.

CHILLINGHAM

11 miles NW of Alnwick off the B6348

Chillingham is a pleasant estate village best known for the herd of wild, horned white cattle that roam parkland close to Chillingham Castle. Descendants of the cattle that once roamed Britain's forests, they are the only herd of wild white cattle in the country. Chillingham village was built by the Earls of Tankerville and contains many Tudor style houses.

Chillingham Castle is beautifully sited within a 365-acre park. Begun in 1245, the castle belonged for many years to the Grey family who fought many battles with the Scots and the Percy's of Alnwick. Sadly the castle fell into ruin in the 1930s, but was bought in the 1980s by Sir Humphrey Wakefield, a descendant of the Grey family, and has been

Chillingham Wild Cattle Park

splendidly restored. Attractions include the impressive Grand Hall, a jousting course, dungeon and torture chamber. The castle and surrounding gardens are open to the public from May to September. Two signposted walks have been laid out through Chillingham Woods, giving superb views over the surrounding countryside.

ELLINGHAM

7 miles N of Alnwick off the A1

Ellingham is a small agricultural village centred on St Maurice's Church, whose Norman details were all but swept away in a restoration of 1862. It features a central tower instead of the more usual west one. Ellingham Hall stands at the end of a quiet lane beyond the village.

CHATHILL

8 miles N of Alnwick off the A1

Close to Chathill is **Preston Tower**, built by Sir Robert Harbottle, Sheriff of Northumberland, in

•

Just outside Chillingham is the National Trust-owned hill fort Ros Castle, once a vital beacon site visible as far afield as the Scottish hills and Holy Island. The whole area was thrown into chaos in 1804 when an over-enthusiastic warden lit the beacon by mistake.

•

88 THE PACK HORSE INN

Ellingham

Interesting seasonal food served every lunchtime and evening in a delightful country inn with five guest bedrooms and a self-contained cottage.

 see page 136

79

Craster

The BBC Gardeners' World
magazine rated Howick
Gardens as one of the top 5
coastal gardens in the
country, and the
Independent Magazine
featured it as 'One of the 10
best gardens to visit in
spring'.

 see page 137

1392. The outside walls are seven
feet thick, whilst inside are fine
tunnel-vaulted rooms which have
changed little over the centuries.
Two turret rooms have been simply
furnished in the style of the period
and there are displays depicting the
Battle of Flodden and life in the
Borders at the start of the 15th
century.

CRASTER

6 miles NE of Alnwick off the B1339

Craster is a small, unpretentious
fishing village with a reputation for
the best oak-smoked kippers in the
country. At one time, herring were
caught around this coast in vast
quantities, but a combination of
over-fishing and pollution resulted
in a decline in numbers, so the fish
now have to be imported. During
the kipper curing season, visitors
can peer into the smoking sheds
where the herring are hung over
smouldering piles of oak chips.

South of Craster is **Howick
Hall**, built in 1782 and long

associated with the Grey family
whose family lineage includes many
famous public figures – most
notably the 2nd Earl Grey, the
great social reformer and tea
enthusiast. The grounds include
wonderful herbaceous borders, a
bog garden, magnificent spring
bulbs and a 65-acre arboretum
planted with thousands of trees and
shrubs planted in six geographical
groups.

Craster Quarry was closed in
1939 and is now a small nature
reserve called the Arnold
Memorial Site. It was this quarry
that supplied London and other
large cities with its kerbstones.
This is the starting point for a
pleasant walk along the coastal
footpath to Dunstanburgh Castle,
or south to Howick, where you
will find the site of a Mesolithic
house. A reconstruction of the
house stands on the cliffs.

EMBLETON

8 miles NE of Alnwick on the B1339

The dramatic ruins of
Dunstanburgh Castle stand on a
clifftop east of the village, on a site
that was originally an Iron Age fort.
The fabric of the castle as seen
today was built in 1313 by Thomas,
Earl of Lancaster, and in the Wars
of the Roses it withstood a siege
from troops led by Margaret of
Anjou, Henry VI's Queen. The
damage caused by the siege was
never repaired, and the castle
remains ruinous to this day.

The castle can't be reached by
road, but a path from the village
passing through Dunstan Steads, a

Craster Harbour

mile southeast of Embleton, leads to it. The Castle, plus the whole coastline to the north as far as Brunton Burn, is owned by the National Trust.

To the north of Embleton is the village of Newton-by-the-Sea, where there are some attractive 18th century fishermans' cottages built around three sides of a square.

BEADNELL
10 miles NE of Alnwick on the B1340

Beadnell is a small fishing village with a harbour and some important 18th-century lime kilns that are now owned by the National Trust. Running eastwards from the harbour into the sea is Ebb's Nook, a narrow strip of land with the scant remains of 13th century **St Ebba's Chapel**, dedicated to the sister of King Oswald, King of Northumbria. This is a delightful stretch of coast, and keen walkers can follow the coastline either by shore path or along the B1340 past St Aidan's Dunes (owned by the National Trust) to Seahouses.

SEAHOUSES
13 miles NE of Alnwick on the B1340

Seahouses is a lively fishing port and small resort with an interesting harbour, magnificent beaches and sand dunes stretching for miles on either side of the town. It is conveniently situated for viewing the Farne Islands, which lie between two and five miles off the coast, and visitors can take a boat trip departing from the harbour to see them at close hand.

Dunstanburgh Castle, nr Embleton

BERWICK-UPON-TWEED

England's northernmost town sits midway between Edinburgh and Newcastle. The River Tweed serves as the border between Scotland and Northumberland along much of its length, but a few miles to the west of Berwick, the border takes a curious lurch north, and curls up and over the town to the east before reaching the coast. So, while Berwick is on the north bank of the Tweed, it's well and truly within Northumberland.

For centuries, this former Royal burgh of Scotland was fought over by the Scots and the English, and changed hands no less than 14 times until it finally became part of England in 1482. But even now, Scotland exerts a great influence. The local football team, Berwick Rangers, plays in the Scottish League, and in 1958 the Lord Lyon,

---

90 CARA HOUSE

Berwick-upon-Tweed

A very cosy, friendly guest house close to the centre of Berwick.

🛏 see page 137

91 BERWICK BARRACKS

Berwick-Upon-Tweed

At Berwick Barracks you and your family can experience military life first hand.

🏛 see page 138

Berwick's original medieval walls were built in the 13th century by Edward I. They were subsequently strengthened by Robert the Bruce when he recaptured the town in 1318, and finally rebuilt by Italian engineers at the bequest of Elizabeth I between 1558 and 1569. They are regarded as being the finest preserved fortifications of their time in Europe. The walk around the walls (about 1.5 miles) provides fine views of the town and the Northumberland coastline. Berwick-upon-Tweed Main Guard is an 18th century neo-classical military guardhouse developed as an interpretive centre for Berwick's walls and fortifications.

who decides on all matters armorial in Scotland, granted the town a coat-of-arms – the only instance of armorial bearings being granted in Scotland for use in England.

But for many years after becoming English, the town was a curious anomaly. In the 16th century Berwick was declared a free burgh, neither in Scotland nor in England, a situation that lasted right up until 1885. Its ambiguous status was such that when war was declared on Russia in 1853, it was done in the name of "Victoria, Queen of Great Britain, Ireland, Berwick-upon-Tweed and all the British Dominions". When peace was announced in 1856, no mention was made of Berwick. So technically, the town remained at war with Russia.

The situation was rectified in 1966, when a Soviet official made a goodwill visit to the town, and a peace treaty was signed. During the ceremony, the Berwick mayor told the Soviet official that the people of Russia could at last sleep easy in their beds.

Berwick's strategic location led it to become an important military town. For many years the garrison soldiers were billeted in local taverns and private houses, but this placed a heavy financial burden on the townspeople. Complaints to the government led to the building of Berwick Barracks between 1717 and 1721. Designed by Nicholas Hawksmoor, they were the first purpose-built barracks in Britain, and within them you'll find the **King's Own Scottish Borderers Museum**. Here visitors will learn about a Scottish regiment that was raised in 1689 by the Earl of Leven, and which is still in existence today. Tel: 01289 304493

Housed in the clock tower of the barracks is the **Berwick-upon-Tweed Museum and Art Gallery**, which explores the history of the town. The museum contains a remarkable collection given to the town by Sir William Burrell, who lived in nearby Hutton Castle. Famous for collecting the works of art that can now be seen in the Burrell Art Gallery in Glasgow, Burrell also donated 300 works of art, sculpture and pottery to Berwick. The Gymnasium Gallery, opened in 1993, displays changing exhibitions of contemporary art. Call 01289 301869 for opening times.

Three distinctive bridges linking the town centre with the communities of Tweedmouth and Spittal span the Tweed estuary. The oldest of these is the 17th-century Berwick Bridge, a handsome stone bridge with 15 arches completed in

Berwick Bridge

1626. The Royal Tweed Bridge is the most modern, having been completed in 1928 with a concrete structure built to an iron bridge design. The enormous 126 feet high, 28 arch Royal Border Bridge, carrying the East Coast main-line railway, was built between 1847 and 1850 by Robert Stephenson.

The Berwick skyline is dominated by the imposing **Town Hall** with its clock tower and steeple that rise to 150 feet, and which is often mistaken for a church. Built between 1754 and 1761, this fine building has a façade as elaborate as its well-documented history. On the ground floor, markets were held in the Exchange and shops and cells existed where now a gift shop and coffee house stand. Guided tours in the summer enable visitors to explore the upper storeys, where there are civic rooms and the former town gaol. A small Cell Block Museum is also located there.

Facing Berwick Barracks is Holy Trinity Church - one of the few Commonwealth churches in England. It was built between 1650 and 1652, during the Commonwealth of Oliver Cromwell, to replace a dilapidated medieval church, which stood on the same site.

AROUND BERWICK-UPON-TWEED

TWEEDMOUTH

1 mile S of Berwick off the A1

Tweedmouth and Spittal, on the English side of the Tweed estuary, are largely suburbs of Berwick. In mid-July a ceremony is held in Tweedmouth, dating back to 1292, to celebrate the fact that the River Tweed, one of the best salmon rivers in Britain, reaches the sea here. The local schools hold a ballot to elect a Salmon Queen, and her crowning marks the beginning of Feast Week which centres on a church service and involves lots of festivities including a traditional salmon supper.

LOWICK

8 miles S of Berwick on the B6353

Lowick is a quiet farming community which contains only a few shops and a couple of pubs. About a mile east of the village are the earthworks of a former castle. The Norman church was replaced by the present St John the Baptist Church.

LINDISFARNE, OR HOLY ISLAND

10 miles SE of Berwick off the A1

Northumberland's northern coastline is dominated by Holy Island, also known by its Celtic name of Lindisfarne. The island is accessible only at low tide, via a 3 mile-long causeway linking it with the mainland at Beal. Tide tables are published locally and are displayed at each end of the road. There are refuges part ways along for those who fail to time it correctly.

As you cross, note the 11th-century Pilgrims' Way, marked by stakes, still visible about 200 metres south of the modern causeway.

On the northwest side of the town you will find all that remains of Berwick Castle. Built in the 13th century, it was demolished in 1850 to make way for the railway station, and the platform now occupies the site of the former Great Hall. The ruins are in the care of English Heritage. The Berwick-upon-Tweed Ramparts comprise gateways, curtain walls and projecting bastions built in 1558 to 1570 to replace earlier defences.

92 LINDISFARNE PRIORY

Lindisfarne

Across the causeway on Holy Island, Lindisfarne Priory is one of the Holiest sites in England. The museum depicts life as it was over a millenium ago.

  see page 138

This route was in use until comparatively recent times.

The island was given to St Aidan in AD 635 by Oswald, King of Northumbria. St Aidan and his small community of Irish monks came from Iona to found a base from which to convert northern England to Christianity. This led to the island being called one of the cradles of English Christianity. St Cuthbert came here to teach and the island became a magnet for pilgrims. When he died in AD 687 he was buried in the church. St Cuthbert's island can be reached at low tide from the island and was used by the saint during times of solitude. A cross marks the site of his tiny chapel.

The early monks are remembered for producing some of the finest surviving examples of Celtic art - the richly decorated **Lindisfarne Gospels**, dating from the 7th century. When the island was invaded by Vikings in the 9th century, the monks fled taking their precious gospels with them. These have, miraculously, survived and are now in the safety of the British Museum. Facsimiles are kept on Lindisfarne and can be seen in the 12th century parish church on the island. The monks also took with them St Cuthbert's bones and wandered around for over 100 years with them before eventually finding a safe resting place in Durham.

During the 11th century a group of Benedictine monks settled here, and the ruins of their great sandstone **Lindisfarne Priory** with its Romanesque great pillars can still be explored.

Lindisfarne Castle was established in Tudor times as yet another fortification to protect the exposed flank of Northumbria from invasion by the Scots. In 1902 it was bought by Edward Hudson, the owner of Country Life magazine, who employed the great Edwardian architect Sir Edward Lutyens to rebuild and restore it as a private house. It is now in the care of the National Trust, and the house and its small walled garden are open to the public during the summer months. Tel: 01289 389244

Holy Island is the finishing point for the 62-mile long **St Cuthbert's Way**, a long distance footpath which opened in 1996. The trail begins at Melrose, across the Scottish border, and along the way passes through the Northumberland National Park and the Cheviot Hills.

Lindisfarne Castle

BELFORD

14 miles S of Berwick off the A1

Belford is an attractive village of stone houses whose broad main street contains some interesting old shops and a fine old coaching inn, reflecting the fact that this was once an important town on the Great North Road. Today it is an ideal holiday base, standing on the edge of the Kyloe Hills, where there are some fine walks, and close to the long golden beaches and rocky outcrops of the coast.

St Cuthbert's Cave, to the north of Belford, is only accessible by foot. It is completely natural, and concealed by a great overhanging rock surrounded by woodland. It is believed that the saint's body lay here on its much interrupted journey across Northumbria. From the summit of nearby Greensheen Hill there are superb views of the coast and of the Cheviots to the west.

WAREN MILL

15 miles SE of Berwick on the B1342

Waren Mill is a small village situated on Budle Bay, a large inlet of flats and sand where vast numbers of wading birds and wildfowl come to feed. Caution should be taken when walking on the flats, as sections quickly become cut off at high tide.

BAMBURGH

16 miles S of Berwick on the B1340

The seaside village of Bamburgh is dominated by the magnificent **Bamburgh Castle**, epic in scale, even by the standards of this

Budle Bay

coastline and its abundance of spectacular castles. Situated on a dramatic basalt outcrop on the very edge of the North Sea, it was almost certainly the royal seat of the first kings of Bernicia. The dynasty was founded by the Saxon King Ida in AD 547 and mentioned in the Anglo-Saxon Chronicle. Ida's grandson Ethelfrid united the kingdoms of Bernicia and Deira, and thus created Northumbria, a kingdom that stretched from the Humber to the Forth and was ruled from Bamburgh.

In those days, the castle would have been made of wood – a mighty stockade surrounding a great royal hall, sleeping quarters, stables, workshops and a garrison for troops. Later on, when Northumbria embraced Christianity, chapels would have been added, and the castle would have been an ostentatious declaration of the Northumbrian kings' power and wealth.

The present stone castle covers eight acres and has an imposing

93 BAMBURGH CASTLE

Bamburgh

Bamburgh Castle is still the home of the Armstrong family, and visitors are able to enjoy what has been described as the finest castle in all England

 see page 139

Bamburgh was the birthplace, in 1815, of Grace Darling, who was only 22 years old when she became the international heroine of her day. In 1838 she rowed out with her father from the Longstone Lighthouse in a ferocious storm to rescue the survivors of the steam ship Forfarshire which had foundered on the Farne Island rocks. In the RNLI Grace Darling Museum visitors can see the open boat she used, her dresses, letters and family belongings, along with a treasure trove of commemorative ware from the 1830s to the present day. Open from Tuesday to Sunday and Bank Holidays.

12th century keep around which three baileys were constructed. The castle was extensively rebuilt and restored in the 18th and 19th centuries, latterly by the first Lord Armstrong whose descendants continue to make this their home.

Bamburgh Castle is open to the public, and rooms on display include the Armoury, King's Hall, Court Room, Cross Hall, Bakehouse and Victorian Scullery, with collections of tapestries, ceramics, furniture and paintings. Occupying the former laundry room is an exhibition dedicated to the first Lord Armstrong and his many remarkable engineering inventions in the fields of hydraulics, ships, aircraft and arms. Here, too, are relics of aviation in the Bamburgh Castle Aviation Artefacts Museum. Tel: 01668 214515.

Just offshore are the **Farne Islands**. This small group of 28 uninhabited islands of volcanic Whin Sill rock provides a major breeding sanctuary for migratory seabirds including puffins, guillemots, razorbills, artic and sandwich terns and kittiwakes. They are also home to a large colony of Atlantic Grey seals, which can often be seen from the beach on the mainland.

The islands have important Christian links, as it was on Inner Farne that St Cuthbert died in AD 687. A little chapel was built here in his memory and restored in Victorian times. The nearby Tower House was built in medieval times by Prior Castell, according to legend, on the site of Cuthbert's cell. Boat trips to the Farne Islands leave from the harbour in Seahouses. Landings are permitted on Inner Farne and Staple Island, times are restricted for conservation reasons and advance booking is necessary at busy times of the year.

HORNCLIFFE

4 miles W of Berwick off the A698

The village of Horncliffe, five miles upstream of Berwick, can only be reached by one road that leads into and out of the village, making it feel rather remote. Many visitors are unaware of the existence of the river, but there is nothing more pleasant than wandering down one of the paths leading to the banks to watch the salmon fishermen on a summer's evening.

Not far from Horncliffe, the River Tweed is spanned by the Union Suspension Bridge linking Scotland and England, built in 1820

Bamburgh Beach

by Sir Samuel Browne, who also invented the wrought-iron chain links used in its construction. The graceful structure, 480 feet long, was Britain's first major suspension bridge to carry vehicular traffic, and although not carrying a major road, it is still possible to drive over it.

NORHAM

6 miles SW of Berwick on the B6470

Norham is a neat village on the banks of the Tweed. Up until 1836 the town was an enclave of the County Palatinate of Durham, surrounded by Northumberland on the south, east and west, and Scotland on the north. **Norham Castle** was built in the 12th century by the Bishop of Durham on a site of great natural strength, guarding a natural ford over the river. It withstood repeated attacks in the 13th and 14th centuries and was thought to be impregnable. However, in 1513 it was stormed by the forces of James IV on his way to Flodden and partially destroyed.

Although it was later rebuilt, the castle was again destroyed by the Scots in 1530, and had lost its importance as a defensive stronghold by the end of the 16th century. The castle is now under the care of English Heritage. Tel: 01289 382329

DUDDO

7 miles SW of Berwick on the B6354

Close to the village are the **Duddo Stones**, one of Northumberland's most important ancient monuments. This ancient stone

circle, which now consists of five upright stones over seven feet high, dates back to around 2000 BC, and can only be reached from the village by foot.

TILLMOUTH

9 miles SW of Berwick on the A698

The village of Tillmouth lies along the banks of the River Till, a tributary of the Tweed which is crossed by the 15th-century Twizel Bridge, although a more modern structure now carries the A698 over the river. Up until the building of the 1727 Causey Arch in County Durham, the old Twizel Bridge, with a span of 90 feet, had the largest span of any bridge in Britain. There are some lovely walks here and a well-signed footpath leads to the ruins of Twizel Castle, and the remains of St Cuthbert's Chapel on the opposite bank, dating from the 18th or 19th centuries, but incorporating some medieval stonework.

94 NORHAM CASTLE

Norham

Commanding a vital ford over the River Tweed, Norham was one of the strongest of the border castles.

  see page 138

Norham's Station Museum is located on the former Tweedmouth-Kelso branch line. The museum features the original signal box, booking office, porter's room model railway. Tel: 01289 382217

Norham Castle

Accommodation, Food & Drink and Places of Interest

The establishments featured in this section includes hotels, inns, guest houses, bed & breakfasts, restaurants, cafes, tea and coffee shops, tourist attractions and places to visit. Each establishment has an entry number which can be used to identify its location at the beginning of the relevant chapter or its position in this section.

In addition full details of all these establishments and many others can be found on the Travel Publishing website - www.travelpublishing.co.uk. This website has a comprehensive database covering the whole of Britain and Ireland.

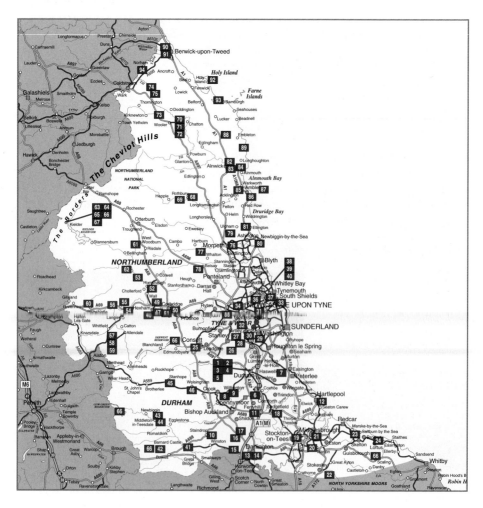

ACCOMMODATION

2 66 Claypath, Durham
6 Old Mill, Metal Bridge, nr Coxhoe
11 Carrsides Farm, Rushyford, nr Ferryhill
13 Balmoral Guest House, Darlington
15 Holme House, Piercebridge, nr Darlington
17 Dog Inn, Heighington, nr Darlington
22 Jet Miners Inn, Great Broughton, nr Stokesley
30 Bowes Incline Hotel, Birtley, nr Gateshead
32 Stables Lodge, Lamesley, nr Gateshead
37 Bell & Bucket, North Shields
39 Lighthouse Guest House, Whitley Bay
42 Clove Lodge, Baldersdale, nr Barnard Castle
46 Ardine Holiday Cottages, Wolsingham, nr Weardale
48 Loughbrow House, Hexham
50 Dyvels Inn, Corbridge
51 Hayes Guest House, Corbridge
52 Greencarts, Humshaugh, nr Hexham
53 Hallbarns Bed & Breakfast, Simonburn, nr Hexham
54 Reading Rooms, Haydon Bridge, nr Hexham
55 Grindon Cartshed, Haydon Bridge, nr Hexham
59 Allendale Tea Rooms, Allendale, nr Hexham
61 Bay Horse Inn, West Woodburn, nr Kielder
63 Twenty Seven B&B, Kielder
65 Leaplish Waterside Park, Kielder
69 The Three Wheat Heads, Thropton
70 Anchor Inn, Wooler
71 Wheatsheaf Hotel, Wooler
73 Red Lion Inn, Milfield, nr Wooler
74 Black Bull, Etal, nr Cornhill on Tweed
77 Dyke Neuk Inn, Meldon, nr Morpeth
79 Micklewood Park, Longhirst, nr Morpeth
81 Hagg Farmhouse B&B, Ellington, nr Morpeth
83 Market Tavern, Alnwick
84 Coach Inn, Lesbury, nr Alnwick
85 Masons Arms, Warkworth, nr Morpeth
88 Pack Horse Inn, Ellingham, nr Chathill
90 Cara House, Berwick-upon-Tweed

FOOD & DRINK

1 La Spaghettata, Durham
6 Old Mill, Metal Bridge, nr Coxhoe
7 Blue House Pub & Restaurant, Haswell, nr Durham
8 Brown Trout, Sunnybrow, nr Crook
9 New Inn, Willington, nr Crook
14 La Sorrentina, Darlington
16 Archer's Jersey Ice Cream, Walworth Gate, nr Darlington
17 Dog Inn, Heighington, nr Darlington
18 Number Four Teashop & Patisserie, Sedgefield
19 Mrs Pattison's Tea Rooms, Stockton-on-Tees
21 Dorman Museum, Middlesbrough
22 Jet Miners Inn, Great Broughton, nr Stokesley
23 Rapps Cafe, Saltburn-by-the-Sea
24 Pie Crust, Loftus, nr Saltburn-by-the-Sea
25 Cricketers, Consett
26 Charlaw Inn, Edmondsley
27 Peggy's Wicket, Beamish Village
29 Washington Wildfowl and Wetlands Centre, Washington
30 Bowes Incline Hotel, Birtley, nr Gateshead
31 Bede's World, Jarrow
37 Bell & Bucket, North Shields
38 Down Under Restaurant, Whitley Bay
41 Bowes Museum, Barnard Castle
43 Countrystyle Bakery & Tea Shop, Middleton-in-Teesdale
45 Baker's Loaf & Old Weardale Tea Rooms, Stanhope, nr Bishop Auckland
47 Bouchon Bistrot, Hexham
49 The Rat Inn, Anick, nr Hexham
50 Dyvels Inn, Corbridge
52 Greencarts, Humshaugh, nr Hexham
56 Vindolanda and Roman Army Museum, Bardon Mill, nr Hexham
57 Golden Lion, Allendale, nr Hexham
58 Allendale Inn, Allendale, nr Hexham
59 Allendale Tea Rooms, Allendale, nr Hexham
60 Pillar Box Café, Haltwhistle, nr Hexham
61 Bay Horse Inn, West Woodburn, nr Kielder
65 Leaplish Waterside Park, Kielder
68 Elm Tree Coffee Shop, Rothbury
69 The Three Wheat Heads, Thropton
70 Anchor Inn, Wooler
71 Wheatsheaf Hotel, Wooler
72 Mojos Cafe Bistro, Wooler
73 Red Lion Inn, Milfield, nr Wooler
74 Black Bull, Etal, nr Cornhill on Tweed
76 The Tower, Morpeth
77 Dyke Neuk Inn, Meldon, nr Morpeth
78 Belsay Hall and Gardens, Belsay, nr Ponteland
80 Nevin's Nibbles, Newbiggin-by-the-Sea
82 The Alnwick Garden, Alnwick
83 Market Tavern, Alnwick
85 Masons Arms, Warkworth, nr Morpeth
86 Cedar Cafe, Amble, nr Morpeth
88 Pack Horse Inn, Ellingham, nr Chathill
89 Howick Hall Gardens and Arboretum, Howick, nr Alnwick
92 Lindisfarne Priory, Lindisfarne
93 Bamburgh Castle, Bamburgh

PLACES OF INTEREST

3 Durham Cathedral, Durham
4 Durham Castle, Durham
5 Crook Hall and Gardens, Durham
10 Raby Castle, Staindrop
12 Hartlepool Historic Quay and Museum, Hartlepool
20 The Captain Cook Birthplace Museum, Marton, nr Middlesbrough
21 Dorman Museum, Middlesbrough
28 Beamish Museum, Beamish Village
29 Washington Wildfowl and Wetlands Centre, Washington
31 Bede's World, Jarrow
33 Arbeia Roman Fort and Museum, South Shields
34 Discovery Museum, Newcastle upon Tyne
35 Path Head Water Mill, Summerhill, nr Blaydon on Tyne
36 Segundum Roman Fort, Baths and Museum, Wallsend
40 St Mary's Lighthouse, Whitley Bay
41 Bowes Museum, Barnard Castle
44 High Force Waterfall, Middleton-in-Teesdale
56 Vindolanda and Roman Army Museum, Bardon Mill, nr Hexham
62 Chipchase Castle, Wark-on-Tyne
64 Kielder Water & Forest Park, Kielder
65 Leaplish Waterside Park, Kielder
66 Go Fishing with Northumbrian Water, Scaling Reservoir
66 Go Fishing with Northumbrian Water, Grassholme and Hury Reservoirs
66 Go Fishing with Northumbrian Water, Cow Green, Selset & Balderhead Reservoirs
66 Go Fishing with Northumbrian Water, Derwent Reservoir
66 Go Fishing with Northumbrian Water, Whittle Dene Lakes
66 Go Fishing with Northumbrian Water, Kielder
66 Go Fishing with Northumbrian Water, Fontburn Reservoir
67 Kielder Water Birds of Prey Centre, Kielder
75 Lady Waterford Hall, Ford, nr Cornhill on Tweed
78 Belsay Hall and Gardens, Belsay, nr Ponteland
82 The Alnwick Garden, Alnwick
87 Coquet Island, Amble, nr Morpeth
89 Howick Hall Gardens and Arboretum, Howick, nr Alnwick
91 Berwick Barracks, Berwick-upon-Tweed
92 Lindisfarne Priory, Lindisfarne
93 Bamburgh Castle, Bamburgh
94 Norham Castle, Norham

1 LA SPAGHETTATA ❚❚

**66 Saddler Street, Durham City,
County Durham DH1 3NP
Tel: 0191 383 9290
website: www.fabiosdurham.com**

Fabio Ciampolillo is the affable owner of **La Spaghettata**, a popular Italian restaurant close to the Castle in the centre of Durham.

Fabio and his staff welcome all their customers into an informal, relaxed setting, with three

main dining areas on the first floor and a bar on the floor above. The menu offers a tempting selection of well-priced dishes, from pizza and pasta to meat, fish and vegetarian favourites accompanied by a good choice of Italian and other wines. La Spaghettata is open for Friday, Saturday and Sunday lunch and every evening.

2 66 CLAYPATH 🛏

**66 Claypath, Durham City,
County Durham DH1 1QT
Tel: 0191 384 3193   mobile: 07974 352372
website: www.66claypath.co.uk**

66 Claypath is a grade II listed Georgian town house, with a delightful secluded garden, in the heart of Durham City. Comfortable, well-furnished rooms are beautifully decorated and quality breakfasts are prepared fresh to order. A short walk from the Market Place, Castle, Cathedral and riverside paths, some of Durham's best restaurants and pubs are within walking distance. Ideally located for exploring not just the

City of Durham but all that the North East has to offer, you can definitely be assured of a warm and friendly welcome.

3 DURHAM CATHEDRAL 🏛

**The College, Durham,
County Durham DH1 3EH
Tel: 0191 386 4266**

In 1093 work began on a magnificent cathedral to house the shrine of St. Cuthbert. The original rib vaulted church, and architectural innovation of great importance, took 40 years to build. Since then the cathedral and St

Cuthbert's shrine have attracted pilgrims and travellers from around the world.

For over nine hundred years the castle and cathedral of St Cuthbert have dominated Durham's skyline. This dramatic panorama is widely regarded as one of the great visual experiences of Europe. Today the castle and cathedral are a World Heritage Site, officially recognising their exceptional quality and character.

4 DURHAM CASTLE 🏛

**Palace Green, Durham,
County Durham DH1 3RW
Tel: 0191 334 3800**

In 1069, three years after landing in Britain, William the Conqueror finally subdued the North of England. William

recognised the defensive potential of the rocky peninsula of Durham and a castle was founded there in 1072. Nine centuries later, **Durham Castle** remains one of England's largest and best-preserved Norman strongholds and one of the grandest Romanesque palaces. Since 1836 it has housed the Foundation College of Durham University, England's third oldest university after Oxford and Cambridge.

5 CROOK HALL AND GARDENS

Sidegate, Durham,
County Durham DH1 5SZ
Tel: 0191 384 8028
e-mail: info@kbacrookhall.co.uk
website: www.crookhallgardens.co.uk

Described by Alan Titchmarsh as 'a tapestry of colourful blooms' **Crook Hall** is a beautiful medieval manor house surrounded by romantic gardens which include ancient fruit trees and climbing roses.

Visitors are invited to try out the maze, hunt down the ghosts, experience the peace and tranquillity of the walled gardens or simply relax and enjoy a homemade cream tea in the pretty little courtyard café.

The Hall is just a short walk from Durham's bustling market place yet the atmosphere is one of peace and tranquillity.

6 OLD MILL

Thinford Road, Metal Bridge,
County Durham DH6 5NX
Tel: 01740 652928 Fax: 01740 657230
e-mail: office@theoldmill.uk.com
website: www.theoldmill.uk.com

Visit Durham and see "the best cathedral on Planet Earth." That's according to world-renowned travel writer Bill Bryson. Bryson fell instantly in love with Durham during a tour of the UK. If, like Bill, you fall in love with Durham, complete the experience by staying in **The Old Mill**.

This former paper mill has recently undergone a dramatic transformation whereby they have created eight of the highest quality en-suite rooms, add to the mix a warm friendly welcome and superb atmosphere and you have one of the best places to stay for miles around.

The Old Mill remains a real pub, where you're just as welcome to enjoy a pint of bitter at the bar as a three-course meal or bar snack. The menu has something for everyone from Jacket Potatoes and Hot Filled Baguettes to Steak and Kidney Suet Pudding, and Gammon Hock with Pork and Bean Hash to Lemon Chicken, all beautifully presented in ample portions.

Set in Metal Bridge, a hamlet in County Durham, The Old Mill is ideally located to explore Durham City, which abounds with things to do. Make time to stroll along the tree-lined riverbank to the themed gardens of Crook Hall or take in the tropical collections of the University's Botanic Gardens. Gourmet treats, original crafts and antique books are just some of the temptations in the specialist shops and markets of Durham city's winding lanes.

Haswell, nr Durham,
County Durham DH6 2AP
Tel/Fax: 0191 526 0307

Geoff Hamilton, his son Craig and Craig's wife Laura are the affable, hardworking hosts at the **Blue House Pub & Restaurant**, which occupies a prominent corner site in the village of Haswell, with lovely views of the countryside on three sides. With a wealth of experience in the trade, they have built up a very successful business by putting the customer first, and their reward is a large and loyal clientele. Customers come from many miles around to enjoy the hospitality, the good company and the excellent food and drink. It's also a popular stop for cyclists (there's a well-used cycle route nearby) and motorists on the busy main A19.

The inn was built of local stone in 1789, and the public rooms retain a traditional ambience assisted by stone walls and some original beams. Food is an increasingly important contributor to the inn's success.

In the bar, in the newly created 50-cover restaurant or in the 30-cover Pemberton Room with its own bar, an extensive menu offers value-for-money meals freshly prepared from seasonal ingredients, locally sourced as far as possible. The printed menu really does offer something for everyone. 'Favourites' include hot beef sandwich, burgers, Cumberland sausage, lasagne, chilli con carne and home-made steak pie. Among the 'House Specialities' are sweet & sour chicken and duck, surf 'n' turf and beef stroganoff. 'From the Sea' come garlic mussels and king prawns, sea bass, salmon and battered or poached cod. Grills come with a choice of five sauces, sizzling dishes add a spicy Cajun or Asian kick and there's always a selection of salads and vegetarian dishes. The main menu is supplemented by lunchtime specials, Sunday roasts and an Early Bird menu. The bar is open from 11am to 11.30pm and food is served lunchtime Monday to Saturday and from 12 to 3 on Sunday for the roasts.

The inn has a delightful sheltered paved patio with smart modern tables and chairs – a real boon in the warmer months. The tarmacked car park includes two bays for disabled drivers next to a ramp access into the bar and restaurant. The restaurant, the patio and the tarmac in the car park are all examples of the family's dedication to improving the inn's amenities, and there will soon be another string to its bow. Craig plans to bring on stream eight en suite bedrooms for B&B guests, which will make it an ideal base for touring a lovely part of the world.

8 THE BROWN TROUT

8 Prospect Place, Sunnybrow, Crook,
County Durham DL15 0NQ
Tel/Fax: 01388 746454
e-mail: theowldtrout@btconnect.com

Landlady Joan Allan is a keen gardener and licensee Barrie Lewins a keen genealogist, but their shared passion is their customers, so a friendly welcome and a good time are guaranteed at the **Brown Trout**. This stone-built, slate-roofed Victorian hostelry stands in the old mining village of Sunnybrow, located on the A690 Durham to Crook road. Hanging baskets and potted plants make a colourful show in the spring and summer, and there are stunning views of the Weardale Valley from the terrace.

Inside, the scene is delightfully traditional, a lovely spot for enjoying locally brewed beers and good conversation. It's equally popular with the local community and with cyclists, walkers, tourists and fishermen: there's good trout fishing nearby, the Weardale Way runs 400 yards away and the pub lies on the Brandon- Bishop Auckland Path. Bar

snacks are served throughout the day and the full menu is available from 5 to 9, with pub classics like sausages & mash, cottage pie, scampi, chilli and spaghetti bolognese – and, naturally, locally caught trout.

On the social side, Tuesday is quiz night, Wednesday it's bingo and there are darts, dominoes and pool events on Saturday. Charity car boot sales are held regularly in the paddock. Families with children and dogs are welcome at the Brown Trout, and there's plenty of off-road parking.

9 THE NEW INN

115 Commercial Street, Willington,
nr Crook, County Durham DL15 0AA
Tel: 01388 748826/747793

In the village and in the trade for 30 years, David and Ann Brunshill took over the **New Inn** in May 2007. The locals and the passing trade – it's on the A688 road from Durham to Weardale – generate a friendly, relaxed feel in the bar, which serves drinks from 11am right through to 1am (11am to midnight on Sunday). A recent extension houses a pool table, and big matches are shown on Sky TV in the bar. At the back of the pub are a car park and a yard where smokers can puff away. Food is only available on Sunday, when a traditional roast lunch is served. Cash only.

Staindrop, County Durham DL2 3AH
Tel: 01833 660202 Fax: 01833 660835
e-mail:rabyestate@rabycastle.com
website: www.rabycastle.com

Raby Castle is not merely a medieval fortress but the home of Lord Barnard. Pass through the Castle gates and be captivated by the historic splendour. Built in the 14th century by the Nevills, most of the interior now dates from the 18th and 19th centuries, although its medieval heart remains. Every room, from the grand Entrance Hall to the Servant's Bedroom gives an insight to life throughout the ages.

Picture the arrival of seven hundred knights gathering in the magnificent Baron's Hall and feel the intrigue of the plotting of the Rising of the North in 1569. Today, see the many treasures including the priceless Meissen birds, part of the beautiful porcelain collection. Throughout the Castle, the many rooms display fine furniture and furnishings, impressive paintings and elaborate architecture for all to see. The kitchen, built in 1360,

remains almost untouched, showing its original medieval form. The cooking equipment has been updated and was in use until 1954.

Wander across the terrace in front of the Castle and look out over the lake to the deer park where 200 Red and 200 Fallow deer graze or take time to enjoy a stroll through the historic gardens. See the formal lawns, ornamental pond and rose garden that are bound by grand yew hedges and towering conifer trees. Look back towards the Castle to admire the magnificent view.

Beyond the gardens you will approach the

18th century Coach Houses which now accommodate the fascinating Coach and Carriage Museum. The Raby State Coach is amongst the finest examples of travel in bygone days. In the Tack Room wonder at the pristine harnesses and trappings. View the original livery worn by the coachman in Edwardian times.

Pause for refreshment and light snacks at the enticing Stable Tea Rooms, where old stalls of the coach horses have been incorporated to create a unique setting. Walk through to the gift shop to buy a present or a memento of your delightful visit to Raby Castle.

12 HARTLEPOOL HISTORIC QUAY & MUSEUM

Jackson Dock, Maritime Avenue,
Hartlepool TS24 0XZ
Tel: 01429 860006 Fax: 01429 867332
e-mail: historic.quay@hartlepool.gov.uk
website: www.thisishartlepool.com

Open every day all year round and voted one of the top six Heritage & History attractions in the UK, **Hartlepool Historic Quay and Museum** is a fun day out for all the family. Here you will find a re-creation of an 18th century seaport which tells the story of life at sea at the time of Captain Cook, Nelson and the Battle of Trafalgar. As well as the coffee shop and gift shop, authentic reconstructions of harbour-side shops surround the Quay, including gunsmiths, tailors and instrument makers. A film presentation shows how two brothers were pressganged into serving aboard ship

and 'Fighting Ships' lets you experience the noise and drama of a naval sea battle.

Guided tours are available of HMS Trincomalee, launched in Bombay in 1817. The oldest floating warship in Britain, it has been lovingly restored at Hartlepool Historic Quay.

The Museum tells the story of Hartlepool from prehistoric times to the present day and includes exhibits such as sea monsters, a Celtic 'Roundhouse', the first 'gas illuminated lighthouse', models, computer interactive displays and PSS Wingfield - a fully restored Paddle Steamer.

---

11 CARRSIDES FARM

Rushyford, County Durham DL17 0NJ
Tel/Fax: 01388 720252
e-mail: carrsides@farming.co.uk

A warm welcome awaits visitors to the 390-acre **Carrsides Farm**. Keith, Liz and their two sons are all involved in running the farm, and next to the farmhouse **West Cottage** provides a homely base for touring the area. The Cottage has two en suite bedrooms, a large living/dining area and a separate kitchen. Guests have the use of a large garden and are free to roam around the farm – children will love meeting the cows, dogs, geese, hens and the peacocks. Quiet and secluded, the farm is nevertheless close to the main road network – the A1(M), J59 or 60, is

a short drive away. The Cottage is let on a self-catering basis, but breakfasts and evening meals are available on request.

---

13 BALMORAL GUEST HOUSE

63 Woodland Road, Darlington,
County Durham DL3 7BQ
Tel: 01325 461908
e-mail: andrew.wise@hotmail.co.uk
website: www.balmoralguest-house.co.uk

In the quiet West End of Darlington, a short stroll from the centre, **Balmoral Guest House** has nine comfortably appointed bedrooms, seven with en suite facilities, ranging from singles to a family room. Privately owned and run by Andrew Wise, the handsome Victorian building is a convenient base for tourists and an ideal stopover for motorists en route to or from Scotland – the A68 is close by and the A1(M) just ten minutes away. A full English breakfast makes the perfect start to the day. Families with children and dogs are welcome. No credit cards.

14 LA SORRENTINA

77-79 Parkgate, Darlington,
County Durham DL1 1RR
Tel/Fax: 01325 467991
website: www.lasorrentina.co.uk

A native of the lovely town of Sorrento, Peppe Termino brought a lifetime's experience in the restaurant and hospitality business when he opened **La Sorrentina** in 2003 in the heart of town next to the Civic Theatre.

Peppe and his Italian staff create a particularly friendly and inviting ambience in the two-floor restaurant, which has won a number of awards, including a 2008 Customer Excellence Award for outstanding contribution to the pursuit of excellent food and service. A variety of menus provide an extensive choice of authentic Italian dishes freshly prepared from top-quality ingredients. Seafood is a speciality, but everything is excellent, from pizza and pasta to chicken and meat dishes, accompanied by a good list of Italian wines.

La Sorrentina is open Thursday to Sunday lunchtimes (roasts on Sunday, must pre-book) and every evening. Happy hour from 5.30 to 7 Sunday to Friday offers special deals on pizza, pasta and chicken dishes with a drink. Bookings are welcomed (advisable at the weekend) and the restaurant accepts the major credit cards. A takeaway service is available. Ample parking nearby – free after 6pm.

15 HOLME HOUSE

Piercebridge, nr Darlington,
County Durham DL2 3SY
Tel/Fax: 01325 374280
e-mail: graham.holmehouse@gmail.com
website: www.holmehouse.com

Anne Graham welcomes Bed & Breakfast guests to **Holme House**, her handsome late-18th century farmhouse in a quiet rural setting close to the Yorkshire border. The centrally heated house, which stands at the heart of a mixed arable and livestock farm, has five

fresh, bright letting bedrooms – three twins (two en suite) and two singles. Guests can relax and plan their days in the sitting room, and the walled garden is a perfect spot for a stroll on a summer evening. Breakfast, full English or Continental, is served at a large pine table in the dining room. Children are welcome, but no pets please. No credit cards. Open all year.

Looking for:
- *Places to Visit?*
- *Places to Stay?*
- *Places to Eat & Drink?*
- *Places to Shop?*

COUNTRY LIVING RURAL GUIDES
HIDDEN INNS
HIDDEN PLACES
COUNTRY Pubs & Inns
off the motorway 3rd edition
www.travelpublishing.co.uk

16 ARCHER'S JERSEY ICE CREAM

New Moor Farm, Walworth Gate,
nr Darlington, County Durham DL2 2UD
Tel: 01325 300336
e-mail: susan@newmoorfarm.co.uk
website: www.archersjerseyicecream.com

The ice cream parlour at New Moor Farm sells some of the finest ice cream you'll ever taste. The Archer family has farmed at Walworth Gate since 1976, but in 2001 their entire herd of Holstein Friesians was wiped out by foot and mouth. John, Susan and their three children started again with a herd of some 300 Jersey cows producing the very best milk and in 2004 they diversified by setting up **Archer's Jersey Ice Cream** as a way of adding value to the milk. They converted two garages and an old forge to make the parlour selling their marvellous product between 10am and 6pm (to 5 in winter).

Besides the creamy, delicious main attraction, with flavours ranging from classic vanilla to banana, liquorice, honey & ginger, strawberry, champagne rhubarb, hokey pokey and Christmas pudding, the parlour sells home-made cakes and

pastries, special occasion ice cream cakes, coffees, teas, smoothies and fresh fruit juices – and, naturally, full-fat and semi-skimmed Jersey milk and cream.

There are seats inside and outside, a children's play area and a two-mile farm walk with sweeping views of the surrounding countryside. New Moor Farm is located just off the A68 northwest of Darlington. The Archers' second parlour is at The Station, Richmond, open from 10.30am to 7.30pm (winter 11.30am to 6.30pm).

17 THE DOG INN

Cross Lane Ends, Heighington,
nr Darlington, County Durham DL2 2TX
Tel: 01325 312152
website: www.doga68.com

Dawn and Dave are a welcoming, enthusiastic couple with a passion for their business. Their pub, **The Dog Inn**, stands just outside the village of Heighington, six miles northwest of Darlington. It's a great favourite with the local community, and with the main A68 road to Weardale and across the border outside it's also a popular stop for motorists and tourists, whether it's for a drink, a snack, a meal or an overnight or longer stay. Dating from the early 1800s, The Dog has a handsome, ivy-clad façade and a cosy, traditional interior with original features including a fine fireplace and some attractive stained glass.

Three real ales, two from local breweries, are on tap in the three-sided bar, and here or in the separate dining area food is a growing part of the pub's trade. Bar snacks and full meals, home-cooked from local

produce, are served every lunchtime and Monday to Saturday evenings.

Accommodation at The Dog comprises two twin-bedded rooms and a single, all with en suite facilities. To the rear of the pub, 12 acres of grounds provide a perfect pull-in for campers and caravanners. On the social side, the pub hosts regular quiz and live music evenings, darts matches and events through the in-house charity club.

18 NUMBER FOUR TEASHOP & PATISSERIE

**4 High Street, Sedgefield,
County Durham TS21 2AU
Tel: 01740 623344**

Sedgefield off the A689, boasts the beautiful St. Edmunds Church as part of the "Heritage Trail" around the charming central green. Also with its National Hunt Racecourse, and Hardwick Country Park on the outskirts, Sedgefield is a "stones throw" from the A1M (junction 60 to the West), and the "National Cycle Route" (Castle Eden Walkway to the East). Sedgefield is popular and central place from which to explore the beautiful coast and rolling farmland of South Durham (Land of the Prince Bishops.), North Yorkshire, and the Durham Dales.

In the centre of this picturesque small town lies, **Number Four Teashop & Patisserie**. Opened on the 29th June 1994, Number Four is a family run teashop that has grown in the hearts and minds of the community of customers who visit us regularly. Linda, Philip, Richard & "the Team" welcome old and new customers alike, to enjoy the traditional qualities of service and value for money which "Number Four" has gained widespread popularity. Most regional savouries and speciality pastries being freshly made on the premises from superior seasonal ingredients, sourced locally. Choose from delicious light meals, sandwiches and quality ice creams. "Eat in" or "Take Away"

Children are welcome and there is assisted wheelchair access. Secure exterior fastenings for cycles & pets. Open 9am to 6pm Mondays to Saturdays inclusive and 10am to 4pm Sundays & Bank Holidays.

19 MRS PATTINSON'S TEA ROOMS

**14 High Street,
Stockton-on-Tees TS18 1UB
Tel: 01642 674727**

There's no more pleasant place in Stockton to pause for refreshment than **Mrs Pattinson's Tea Rooms**. Owner Ann Pattinson loves the town and loves its people, and the large and loyal band of regulars show that the feeling is mutual. The smartly appointed tea rooms in the heart of town, with neat linen on the tables and local artwork on the walls, are open from 9 to around 3 Monday to Saturday for cooked-to-order breakfasts, traditional lunches, salads and home baking. Children are welcome. Guide dogs only. No credit cards.

21 DORMAN MUSEUM

**Linthorpe Road, Middlesbrough TS5 6LA
Tel: 01642 813781
website: www.dormanmuseum.co.uk**

The Dorman Museum re-opened on the 1st March 2003 after a three year programme of major alterations and construction. The museum now offers five new galleries housing permanent and temporary exhibitions and an enjoyable,

accessible environment in which to learn something new. The museum houses outstanding ornithological, archaeological and ceramic and decorative Arts collections. There's always something for everyone including plenty of hands-on activities, objects and children's trails.

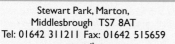

20 THE CAPTAIN COOK BIRTHPLACE MUSEUM

Stewart Park, Marton,
Middlesbrough TS7 8AT
Tel: 01642 311211 Fax: 01642 515659
e-mail:
captcookmuseum@middlesbrough.gov.uk
website: www.captcook-ne.co.uk

The Captain Cook Birthplace Museum forms part of Middlesbrough Museums & Galleries Service along with its sister venue - the Dorman Museum, situated in Linthorpe Road close to Albert Park. The Service has also developed a new modern art gallery, called **mima** (Middlesbrough Institute of Modern Art), which opened in January 2007.

The museum opened on the 28th October 1978 - the 250th anniversary of Cook's birth. It is housed in a purpose-built building close to the granite urn marking the site of Cook's birthplace cottage in Stewart Park, Marton, Middlesbrough. The museum tells the story of one of the world's greatest navigators and mariners through themed display galleries, temporary exhibitions, associated activities and events and a lively education programme.

There is full disabled access throughout and additional facilities such as the Discovery Room (education & activities), the Endeavour Room (meetings & events), the Resolution Resources Room (archive & research), gift/book shop, and a café.

22 THE JET MINERS INN

61 High Street, Great Broughton, Stokesley,
North Yorkshire TS9 7EF
Tel: 01642 712427
e-mail: david.williams@ntlworld.com

David Williams has a warm welcome for visitors to the **Jet Miners Inn**, a delightful 200-year-old inn located by the B1257 road south of Stokesley.

Coal fires keep things cosy in the all-day bar and lounge, and in the 70-cover restaurant a good variety of hearty home-cooked food is served. The mellow-stone exterior is festooned with hanging baskets and greenery in season, and the inn has a delightful garden with two little ponds. Six comfortable bedrooms with en suite showers provide a civilised, convenient base for a cycling or walking holiday (Great Broughton stands on the 2C2 Coast to Coast path) or for discovering the scenic and historic delights of Captain Cook country and the North York Moors National Park.

23 RAPPS CAFÉ

11 Milton Street, Saltburn-by-the-Sea,
Cleveland TS12 1DH
Tel/Fax: 01287 626323

Behind its floor-to-ceiling window **Rapps Café** is a bright, relaxed spot for enjoying a snack or a meal at any time between 9 in the morning and 9 in the evening. Just a short walk from the promenade and beach, Greg Beatty's licensed café is a popular place with both locals and tourists, the

latter including walkers and cyclists on the Cleveland Way. The menu offers an excellent variety of wholesome, straightforward fare, from panini and jacket potatoes to cakes, pastries and cream teas. Families with children are welcome, and the café accepts the major credit cards. Wheelchair access to the café and toilets.

24 THE PIE CRUST

19 High Street, Loftus,
Saltburn-by-the-Sea,
Cleveland TS13 4HW
Tel: 01287 641111

Vivacious Vicki long cherished an ambition to own and run her own café/coffee shop and the former PE teacher realised that dream when she took over **The Pie Crust** in May 2008. The Grade II listed building is part of a Georgian terrace in the centre of the village of Loftus, which stands five miles south of Saltburn-by-the-Sea on the A174 road to Whitby. The interior is bright, cheerful and unpretentious, with wooden floors, farmhouse-style chairs and fresh flowers on the tables.

Vicki has lost no time in winning over the locals, building up a loyal clientele, and she also has a warm welcome for passing motorists, tourists, walkers and cyclists. Cakes, pastries and pies are baked daily on the

premises, and there's always a good choice of cold and hot dishes, including the popular beef cobbler and the daily roasts. Drinks include a good variety of teas and coffees.

The Pie Crust is open from 9.30 to 4 Monday to Friday and from 10 to 1 on Saturday. It is also open once a month for Sunday lunch (call for times) and evening bookings are taken for groups of 8 or more. No credit cards.

25 THE CRICKETERS

66 Durham Road, Blackhill, nr Consett,
County Durham DH8 5TH
Tel/Fax: 01207 593979
website: www.thecricketersblackhill.co.uk

The Cricketers is a mid-Victorian building on the A691, set in stunning countryside in a conservation area of Derwentside. Hosts Lee and Dawn Shaw, who took over the lease in July 2007, have a warm and genuine welcome for their local clientele and for passing motorists, cyclists and walkers – the inn is right on the Derwent Walk and just ten minutes' drive from the Derwent Reservoir, a much-visited attraction that's rich in wildlife. Behind the slate-roofed stone frontage the inn is tasteful and traditional, with lots of interesting ornaments and memorabilia.

Regularly changing guest ales accompany the resident Black Sheep, and visitors can enjoy them in the cosy lounge, in the beer garden or in the main bar, which has a raised area for pool, darts and entertainment; big-screen TVs show the major sporting events and the inn hosts regular live band or karaoke evenings and a quiz on Monday evenings. Food is limited to a popular Sunday lunch with traditional roasts (bookings are welcomed). Bar hours are 5 to 11 Monday to Thursday, 3 to 12 on Friday, 12 to 12 on Saturday and 12 to 11 on Sunday. No credit cards.

**Blackhouse, Edmondsley,
County Durham DH7 6EH
Tel: 01207 232085**

It takes a good landlord to make a good pub and in David Brown and his partner Tish the **Charlaw Inn** has one of the very best. He brought 25 years' experience in the hospitality business when he took over this, his first venture into the pub trade. They have really put the place back on the map – except literally, that is, as you won't find Blackhouse on most road atlases. It's the name that was originally given to the hamlet that grew up around the pub, which is located close to Edmondsley, on the B6532 that runs between the city of Durham and the town of Stanley.

The busy market town of Chester-le-Street is nearby, and even nearer is Waldridge Fell Country Park, County Durham's last surviving area of lowland heath. The whole area of open countryside is rich in natural history, and the best reward for a spell in the bracing air is a visit to the Charlaw Inn, which takes its name from a local fell. David is a mine of information about local history and he will happily chat with his customers about almost any sport.

Making the customers happy is David and Tish's first priority, and their brick-built, slate-roofed pub, its frontage adorned in spring and summer with colourful hanging baskets, attracts a wide cross-section of regulars: locals from the surrounding communities, families, farmers, walkers, lovers of the countryside and darts players. The public spaces comprise a bar/lounge area with seats for 30, a

conservatory overlooking the garden (30 more seats) and a separate 50-cover à la carte restaurant. There's an indoor family area with a video games player, and children can also have fun on the playslide in the garden. Local produce is the basis for the food, which runs from excellent value bar snacks to the full dining experience in the restaurant. The bars and the restaurant are accessible to wheel chair users. There is also a large car park to the rear that can accomodate 40 cars.

The Charlaw Inn is open from 3 to 11 on Monday (no food) and from midday to 11 on all other days of the week.

27 PEGGY'S WICKET

Station Road, Beamish Village,
Co Durham DH9 6RN
Tel: 0191 370 0384

Peggy's Wicket is a popular dining pub in the heart of Beamish village, a ten-minute walk from the renowned Open Air Museum, and an easy drive from Chester-le-Street and Durham. Run since Easter 2008 by Andrew Brown and Emma Richards, the inn is open from 11am to 11pm every day, attracting a wide cross-section of regular custom as well as cyclists, walkers, tourists and motorists.

In the spacious bar areas an extensive range of real ales, lagers, spirits and soft drinks is served, and there's also a good choice of wines to enjoy on their own or to accompany a snack or a meal. The main menu, available from 11.30 to 6, provides an impressive variety of dishes from pub classics to world dishes, from sandwiches, jacket potatoes and omelettes to gammon steak, mince with dumplings, fish & chips, lemon sole goujons, chicken fajitas, salad platters, succulent steaks and Thai green chicken curry with jasmine rice. There are

separate vegetarian and curry menus and a children's menu (and many of the dishes on the main menu can be ordered in smaller portions). The main menu gives way at 6 to the gourmet menu, where typical dishes might include black pudding topped with a quail egg, tuna steak with a black bean stir fry, fillet steak Wellington or butterflied chicken with a creamy stilton sauce.

Peggy's Wicket holds regular themed food nights (medieval, curry, Spanish) and accepts the major credit cards. There's ample car parking space right across the road.

28 BEAMISH MUSEUM

Beamish, County Durham DH9 0RG
Tel: 0191 370 4000 Fax: 0191 370 4001
e-mail: museum@beamish.org.uk
website: www.beamish.org.uk

No trip to County Durham is complete without a trip to the award-winning **North of England Open Air Museum at Beamish**. Set in 300 acres of countryside, it illustrates life in the North of England in the early 1800s and 1900s. There is so much to see. Stroll down a cobbled street full of shops, banks and offices, visit an old Methodist chapel, find out how life was lived on a farm in the late 19th century, take a trip on a tram or steam train, visit an old dentist's surgery (and be grateful you didn't live in those days, and needed a filling!), walk through a colliery village, and go down a drift mine.

You can also see the world's third oldest surviving railway engine, which dates from 1822, housed in a specially created Great Engine Shed. There's also

Pockerley Manor and Horse Yard, based on a small fortified manor house. Here you experience life as it was lived 200 years ago. Stroll the terraced gardens, walk through the fine horse yard, and see the costumes from all these years ago.

Beamish is justly famous as a great day out for all the family. Reasonably priced meals and snacks are available, and there's a friendly shop where you can buy souvenirs.

29 WASHINGTON WILDFOWL & WETLANDS CENTRE

Washington, Tyne and Wear NE38 8LE
Tel: 0191 416 5454 Fax: 0191 416 5801
e-mail: info.washington@wwt.org.uk
website: www.wwt.org.uk

WWT Washington is one of nine Centres run by the Wildfowl & Wetlands Trust, a registered charity. Here you can have a fantastic day out seeing, feeding and learning about wetland birds, whilst also helping WWT to conserve wetland habitats and their biodiversity.

At the Heron Hides, closed circuit cameras allow you to see individual nests during the breeding season, of the largest colony of Grey Hreons in the area. A variety of ducks, geese and swans can be seen in the reserve, including the Nene, state bird of Hawaii, saved from the brink of extinction by WWT. Having arrived at Washington in 1986, the Chilean Flamingo colony is now breeding well and often makes use of the Flamingo House, built with a donation from author Catherine Cookson. The James Steel Waterfowl Nursery, built in 1996 is the first home for most of the ducks and geese that hatch at Washington and special tours take place during the breeding season.

You can take your time to stroll around the nature reserve, or explore Spring Gill Wood with its ponds, streams and woodland. The Hawthorn Wood Wild Bird Feeding Station attracts a variety of woodland birds such as Woodpeckers and Sparrowhawks that can be seen mostly during the winter. The centre also has an adventure play area for children, a waterside café and The Glaxo Wellcome Discovery Centre, with its displays and exhibits.

30 BOWES INCLINE HOTEL

Northside, Birtley, Gateshead,
Tyne & Wear DH3 1RF
Tel: 0191 410 2233 Fax: 0191 410 4756
e-mail: info@thebowesinclinehotel.co.uk
website: www.thebowesinclinehotel.co.uk

Gateshead has a rich and diverse history just waiting to be discovered. Alongside modern attractions sit architectural treasures and monuments straight out of the history books. You can enjoy all of the above while resting your head at the recently renovated **Bowes Incline Hotel**. The Bowes Incline has it all, magnificent views across the rolling countryside, 18 beautifully decorated en-suite bedrooms, a fully stocked bar with an open log fire and a spacious dining area serving quality restaurant-standard food all within a Hotel setting.

Proud of its heritage the hotel takes its name from the Bowes Incline Railway and Museum, a gem of North Eastern Industrial History, the cosy alcoves within the open-plan dining area are full of pictures and Mining memorabilia making it an interesting and intimate setting in which you can enjoy dishes cooked to order from a menu created to be both appealing and tempting. The full menu is now served all day every day, that means right

through to 9.30pm Monday to Friday, 10.00pm on Saturday, and 9.00pm on Sunday night.

Situated just off the A1 within a short walk of the amazing Angel of the North, and is equally appealing as a place to pause on a journey, a destination restaurant and a base for both tourists and business people alike.

31 BEDE'S WORLD

Church Bank, Jarrow,
Tyne and Wear NE32 3DY
Tel: 0191 489 2106
e-mail: Visitor.info@bedesworld.co.uk
website: www.bedesworld.co.uk

Bede's World celebrates the extraordinary life and achievements of the Venerable Bede (AD 673 – 735) who lived and worked here in the monastery over 1300 years ago. Visit the interactive "Age of Bede" exhibition in the stunning museum building; the site of the Anglo-Saxon monastery of St Paul, and

medieval monastery ruins; rare breeds of animals and reconstructed timber buildings on Gyrwe, the Anglo-Saxon demonstration farm and the attractive herb garden in a tranquil setting.

There is a café within historic Jarrow Hall serving delicious freshly made hot meals, snacks and cakes; gift shop, with a wide range of books, attractive crafts and souvenirs and an outdoor children's play area and picnic tables in nearby Drewett's Park.

32 STABLES LODGE

South Farm, Lamesley, Gateshead, NE11 0ET
Tel: 01914 921756
e-mail: janet@stableslodge.co.uk
website: www.thestableslodge.co.uk

The MacPherson Household would love to welcome you their award winning luxury Bed and Breakfast, **The Stables Lodge**, this year's winner of the prestigious AA award for Guest Accommodation of the Year for England in 2008 – 2009. Situated in a beautiful rural location of Lamesley it is hard to believe that the A1 is just 2 minutes away, thus providing easy access to the cities of Newcastle and Gateshead, the Metro Centre and the Angel of the North. The Lodge is also ideally situated for visiting Beamish Museum and the beautiful City of Durham.

Its unique location and the reputation The Stables has earned make it desirable accommodation for Tourist and Corporate Guests alike. From the moment you arrive you will appreciate being somewhere rather special, where our commitment to making your stay both memorable and enjoyable is genuine and absolute. The Stables was converted by its current owners and benefits from their interior design background – presenting a "Hunting Lodge" Theme

based around warm mellow colours, colourful tartans and a host of facilities designed to enhance your comfort.

The emphasis is on great customer service and relaxation in an informal yet stylish atmosphere where you can pamper yourself and truly feel at home. Bring some indulgence to your day and relax in your private sauna or spa bath (the Red Room) or relax in the tranquillity of your private hot tub (The Garden Room) – our complimentary bathrobes and guest slippers together with our Molton Brown toiletries are on hand to assist with your relaxation.

33 ARBEIA ROMAN FORT & MUSEUM

Baring Street, South Shields,
Tyne and Wear NE33 2BB
Tel: 0191 456 1369 Fax: 0191 427 6862
website: www.twmuseums.org.uk/arbeia

Built around AD160, **Arbeia Roman Fort** once guarded the entrance to the River Tyne, playing an essential role in the mighty frontier system. Based four miles east of the end of Hadrian's Wall at South Shields, the Fort was originally built to house a garrison and soon became the military supply base for the 17 forts along the Wall. Today, the excavated remains, stunning reconstructions of original buildings and finds discovered at the Fort combine to give a unique insight into life in Roman Britain.

35 PATH HEAD WATER MILL

Summerhill, Blaydon on Tyne,
Tyne and Wear NE21 4SP
Tel: 0191 414 6288
e-mail: enquiries@gatesheadmill.co.uk
website: www.gatesheadmill.co.uk

For many years, the 18th century **Path Head Water Mill** lay abandoned and neglected. Then, in 1995, it was decided to restore it to its full working glory. In 1998 it opened to the public, though there is still a lot of work to be done. It is located in a picturesque, quiet dell, and here you can see how water was the main source of energy before the advent of the steam engine, and how a mill harnessed the power of water to turn its machinery. A small gallery of photographs shows you the stages in the mill's restoration, plus there's a tearoom. Opening Times: Tuesday-Sunday 11am-3pm in winter and 10am-5pm in summer; Closed Mondays, except for bank holidays; Admission charge

34 DISCOVERY MUSEUM

Blandford Square, Newcastle upon Tyne,
Tyne and Wear NE1 4JA
Tel: 0191 232 6789 Fax: 0191 230 2614
website: www.twmuseums.org.uk/
discovery

Discovery is the North East of England's most popular free museum. Discover all about life in Newcastle and Tyneside, from the area's renowned maritime history and world-changing science and technology right through to fashion through the eras and military history. The museum is bursting with interactive displays, which makes it the perfect place to learn and have fun. The displays are regularly updated and complemented by an array of free, fun learning activities.

One of the favourite exhibits - Turbinia - dominates the entrance to the Museum. Invented on Tyneside, it is the first ship to be powered by a steam turbine. The 35 metre vessel was once the fastest ship in the world and her history is brought to life in the Turbinia Story display. She sets the standard for a day out that is guaranteed to be filled with breathtaking discoveries.

105

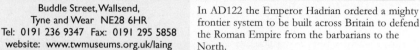

36 SEGEDUNUM ROMAN FORT, BATHS & MUSEUM

Buddle Street, Wallsend,
Tyne and Wear NE28 6HR
Tel: 0191 236 9347 Fax: 0191 295 5858
website: www.twmuseums.org.uk/laing

In AD122 the Emperor Hadrian ordered a mighty frontier system to be built across Britain to defend the Roman Empire from the barbarians to the North.

The result was Hadrian's Wall, a 73 mile barrier stretching from the River Tyne in the east to the Solway Firth in the west. Segedunum, which means strong fort, stood at the eastern end of the Wall and was home to 600 Roman soldiers. For almost 300 years **Segedunum** guarded this important part of the frontier.

Today, Segedunum is once again the gateway to Hadrian's Wall. It is the most excavated fort along the Wall and has a large interactive museum plus a 35 metre high viewing tower providing outstanding views across this World Heritage Site.

37 BELL & BUCKET

37 Norfolk Street, North Shields,
Tyne and Wear NE30 1NQ
Tel: 0191 257 0680

A few minutes from the main square of North Shields, in the traditional part of town, the **Bell & Bucket** can be found. A listed ex fire-station, this inn provides an intimate, homely feel to accompany the home-cooked food and selection of real ales. The dark oak furnishings and the abundance of fishing quay photographs depicting the history and heritage of the area provide a welcome backdrop for the live music and quiz nights. The pub has 5 hotel rooms available, is open daily between 11am and 11pm and encourages children and animals.

38 DOWN UNDER RESTAURANT

7/8 Lower Promenade, Whitley Bay,
Northumberland NE26 1AN
Tel: 0191 253 3876

The **Down Under** is a cheerful eating place on the lower promenade, above the golden sands of Whitley Bay. Inside, the restaurant has the relaxed look of an Australian beach café. Owner-chef Alison Hay, here since 1990, proves that variety is the spice of life with a menu that tours the world, with everything prepared to order from fresh produce in her tiny kitchen. Among the favourite dishes are garlic mushrooms, tacos, burgers and chilli (both meat and vegetarian versions), and daily specials like spicy chicken or Mediterranean lamb. Down Under is open on Wednesday to Saturday evenings and Friday to Sunday lunchtimes. Closed Christmas to Easter.

39 THE LIGHTHOUSE GUEST HOUSE

20 North Parade, Whitley Bay,
Northumberland NE26 1PA
Tel: 0191 252 2319
e-mail: leachgerald@googlemail.com

'Come as a guest, leave as a friend' is the invitation extended by affable host Jerry Leach, who took over the **Lighthouse Guest House** in April

2008. The accommodation comprises five guest rooms – a single, two doubles, another double with a Z-bed and a family room with a double bed, two single beds and a cot. All the rooms have television, free wifi connection and a hot beverage tray, and guests start the day with a hearty breakfast served in the dining room.

This substantial Victorian property, recently smartly refurbished by Jerry, enjoys a quiet location just 200 yards from the promenades, the golden sands and the sea, and is equally convenient for shops, restaurants and pubs.

This stretch of the Northumbrian coast, including Tynemouth and Cullercoats as well as Whitley Bay, is a great place for a holiday, with a variety of things to do for all the family. Whitley Bay itself has a thriving night life and hosts an annual international jazz festival, and visitors who climb to the top of St Mary's Lighthouse are rewarded with stunning views. The Lighthouse, which is open all year round, offers excellent value for money and has excellent off-road parking.

40 ST MARY'S LIGHTHOUSE

St Mary's Island, Whitley Bay,
Tyne and Wear NE26 4RS
Tel: 0191 200 8650

Just north of Whitley Bay, you'll find **St Mary's Lighthouse** and the adjoining keepers' cottages, situated on a small island which is accessible at low tide. It was built in 1898, and closed in 1984. Now it has been converted into a fascinating small museum and visitor centre by North Tyneside Council. There are 137 steps to the top, though the climb is worth it - the views are spectacular! If the climb doesn't appeal, you can still see it courtesy of a video at ground level. An exhibition explains the history of the lighthouse and the varied wildlife of the island, which is a nature reserve. There's also a small souvenir shop, and plenty of parking on the mainland. Opening times: Depends on tides; phone for leaflet; Admission charge.

HIDDEN PLACES GUIDES

Explore Britain and Ireland with *Hidden Places* guides - a fascinating series of national and local travel guides.

Packed with easy to read information on hundreds of places of interest as well as places to stay, eat and drink.

Available from both high street and internet booksellers

For more information on the full range of *Hidden Places* guides and other titles published by Travel Publishing visit our website on

www.travelpublishing.co.uk
or ask for our leaflet by phoning
01752 276660 or emailing
info@travelpublishing.co.uk

41 BOWES MUSEUM

Barnard Castle, County Durham DL12 8NP
Tel: 01833 690606 Fax: 01833 637163
e-mail: info@bowesmuseum.org.uk
website: www.bowesmuseum.org.uk

The Bowes Museum is one of County Durham's great surprises - a beautiful and grand French chateau-style museum on the outskirts of the historic town of Barnard Castle. It was built by John Bowes, illegitimate son of the 10th Earl of Strathmore, and his Parisian actress wife, Josephine, Countess of Montalbo, between 1862 and 1875. They wanted to house the vast collection of works of art they had amassed from all corners of Europe so that people from all walks of life could see and enjoy them, but unfortunately they died before their dream was realised.

But realised it eventually was, and today it has an outstanding collection that will take your breath away. Here the visitor can admire a vast range of objets d'arts and paintings, including what is acknowledged to be the most important collection of Spanish paintings in Britain. But John and Josephine Bowes didn't just restrict themselves to the grand and the prestigious. There is also a wonderful display of toys, including the world's first toy train set.

The Museum's most famous exhibit is undoubtedly the Silver Swan. The life-sized bird, with its exquisite silver plumage, is an automaton and musical box, set in a stream made from twisted glass rods with small fish "swimming" among them. When it is wound up, the glass rods rotate, a tinkling tune is played, and the swan preens itself before lowering its head towards the water and seemingly picking up a fish. It then raises its head once more and appears to swallows it.

The licensed café sells snacks and light meals, and there's a shop where you can buy a souvenir or gift. Parking is free, and, apart from one or two areas, the museum is disabled-friendly. There are also 23 acres of gardens and parkland to enjoy.

42 CLOVE LODGE

Baldersdale, Barnard Castle,
County Durham DL12 9UP
Tel/Fax: 01833 650030
e-mail: carolinecarter69@aol.com
website: www.clovelodge.co.uk

Caroline Carter had always had a yen to own a farm, and she chose a wonderful part of the world when she acquired a twenty-acre livestock farm on the edge of the fells. **Clove Lodge**, which stands next to the farmhouse, is a Victorian stone-built, slate-roofed cottage with accommodation on two floors. On the ground floor are an en suite double/twin bedroom, a large, comfortable sitting room, a well-equipped kitchen and a cosy dining room. Upstairs is a double bedroom with its own bath/shower room.

The cottage has an attractive south-facing area with tables, chairs and a small barbecue overlooking a wooded dale, waterfall and stream. Peace, solitude and the dramatic scenery of the North Pennines attract a wide cross-section of visitors, including tourists, walkers, cyclists, anglers (there's excellent fishing on nearby reservoirs) and wedding guests at the wonderful Bowes Museum.

Barnard Castle is a short drive away, and other places of interest in the vicinity include high and Low Force waterfalls, Raby Castle and the villages of Romaldkirk and Cotherstone. The two rooms at Clove Lodge can be let separately or the cottage let as a whole, for either Bed & Breakfast (with evening meals by arrangement) or self-catering; for the latter, fresh eggs and lamb from the farm can be supplied. No credit cards. Caroline also offers basic, rustic accommodation for guests in a converted barn – ideal for a group of walkers or cyclists.

43 COUNTRY STYLE BAKERY & TEA SHOP

No 20 Market Place, Middleton-in-Teesdale,
County Durham DL12 0QG
Tel: 01833 640924
e-mail: mail@countrystylebakery.co.uk
website: www.countrystylebakery.co.uk

David, formerly in IT, and Hazel, in catering for 30 years, combine their talents in running the **Country Style Bakery & Tea Shop** on the market place of Middleton-in-Teesdale. Behind the sturdy stone frontage the interior is light, bright and roomy, with smart modern pine tables and chairs. Hazel prepares an excellent selection of sweet and savoury

delights that attract a wide cross-section of visitors, from locals and families to walkers, cyclists, bikers and motorists. It's also a popular spot with the many tourists who come from near and far to Middleton-in-Teesdale, a small town that's a pleasant place to explore and a convenient centre from which to discover the superb scenery and natural sights of the region.

Savoury options include a full lunch menu, jacket potatoes, panini's and quiches. For the sweeter tooth

there's always a tempting array of home baking, typically including coffee cake, chocolate cake, saucy tart (one of our specialities), lemon drizzle, fruit pies and egg custards. Drinks include a good selection of hot and cold drinks, including coffee from freshly ground beans. Most of the items on the tea shop menu can be taken away from the bakery.

Opening hours are 9 to 5 Monday to Saturday, 10.30 to 5 on Sunday. Telephone bookings taken. No credit cards. The bakery and tea shop and the toilets are accessible to wheelchair users.

44 HIGH FORCE WATERFALL

Enquiries to Raby Estate Office,
Middleton-in-Teesdale,
County Durham DL12 0QH
Tel: 01833 640209 Fax: 01833 640963
e-mail: teesdaleestate@rabycastle.com

From its rise as a trickle, high on the heather covered fells at the top of the North pennines, to the top of the whin sill rock at Forest-in-Teesdale, the River Tees steadily grows and gathers pace. Then it suddenly and spectacularly drops 70 feet. **High Force** is reputed to be the highest unbroken fall of water in England. You'll feel its awesome power as you begin the approach. There's the peace and quiet of the countryside, but something else - an air of anticipation.

As you begin the descent down the gently sloping, well-maintained path, a muffled rumble reaches your ears. You can enjoy the pretty woodland walk which twists and turns with a different view every few yards, but still the waterfall escapes you. Then the rumble turns into a roar - you can imagine the feel of spray on your face and there's a natural earthy aroma. You peer through the trees and there it is. The sight astounds you. Postcards and photographs can't portray the sheer size of the vertical wall of water - the ceaseless roaring sound - and the almost tangible atmosphere of the place. High Force commands respect. Its power is its beauty, but it must be treated with care. Children should be supervised at all times. High Force is open all year and is spectacular throughout the seasons.

45 THE BAKER'S LOAF & WEARDALE TEA ROOMS

37 Front Street, Stanhope,
Bishop Auckland, County Durham DL13 2TS
Tel: 01388 526113

A fine Weardale stone building with sash windows and a tiled roof is home to the **Baker's Loaf & Weardale Tea Rooms**. Owner Diane Wright has built up a large and loyal local following since she came here in 1996, and she also welcomes visitors to this interesting little town in the centre of Upper Weardale.

All the food is prepared on the premises and among the favourite orders to eat in or take away are super made-to-order sandwiches (try the beef or pork with stuffing), quiches, omelettes, plated salads, all-day breakfasts and excellent pies – steak or chicken, leek & mushroom. For those with a sweeter tooth the tea room always has a selection of cakes, scones, home-made preserves and honeys and Mövenpick ice creams. Diane's speciality cream teas, served from 2 o'clock, are a treat not to be missed.

Most of the seats are upstairs, but there are four on the ground floor and 12 more in the garden, where there's an area for children to play. The Bakery & tea Room is open from 8 to 4.30 Monday to Saturday and from 10 to 4 on Sunday. It's a lovely place for a party or other celebration, and special cakes can be ordered to mark the occasion.

46 ARDINE HOLIDAY COTTAGES

Melbourne Place, Wolsingham, Weardale,
County Durham DL13 3EQ
Tel: 01388 527538
website: www.ardinehcottages.co.uk

Owned and run by local couple Ian and Marj Gardiner, **Ardine Holiday Cottages** are two 19th century stone terraced properties overlooking a little green in the old part of Wolsingham. Both are cosy and traditional, with two bedrooms, a comfortable living room, well-equipped kitchen and small enclosed yards at the back. Wolsingham, the gateway to Weardale, is surrounded by lovely countryside, with miles of footpaths and easy access to many tourist and leisure attractions, including Tunstall Reservoir (excellent fishing), Hamsterly Forest and the Weardale railway. The self-catering cottages are available throughout the year. No credit cards.

47 BOUCHON BISTROT

4 – 6 Gilesgate, Hexham,
Northumberland NE46 3NJ
Tel: 01434 609 943
e-mail: info@bouchonbistrot.co.uk
website: www.bouchonbistrot.co.uk

Situated in a handsome Grade II listed building, **Bouchon Bistrot** in Hexham offers a touch of classic French cuisine in elegant, sophisticated and relaxing surroundings. Award winning Restauranteur Gregory Bureau and his wife Clare manage to provide a traditional French menu at attractive prices.

Greg, who learnt his trade in several Michelin-starred restaurants in France, creates simple, traditional recipes with good quality produce. The restaurant itself is decorated with a French bistrot in mind with wooden floors, original Oak beams and open fires on each of the restaurant's three levels. The French bistrot feel is continued with French music playing and the menu is in French and English.

The rustic menu created by Chef Nicolas Duhil contains mouth watering dishes such as Assiette De Charcuterie, Red Wine Monkfish 'Matelote', French Onion Soup and Crispy Duck Confit. The food has been critically acclaimed, with the restaurant being reviewed in the Good Food Guide. With the Bouchon Bistrot growing in popularity all the time, reservations are recommended, children are welcome and there is full disabled access.

Opening Hours: Tues to Sat, Lunch: 12pm – 2pm; Dinner: 6pm – 9.30pm; Sunday Lunch: 12pm – 3pm; Early Bird Special: Tues to Fri, 6pm – 7pm

49 THE RAT INN

Anick, Hexham,
Northumberland NE46 4LN
Tel: 01434 602 814
e-mail: info@theratinn.com
website: www.theratinn.com

Situated in the picturesque hamlet of Anick, about 1 mile from the historical market town of Hexham, the **Rat Inn** boasts spectacular views over Hexham and across the Tyne Valley. Karen and Phil are both experienced in the trade

and took over the Rat in September 2007 and due to Phil's expertise in the kitchen the Inn has been featured in the Michelin Eating out in Pubs 2009, as well as the Good Pub Guide 2008 and the Good Beer Guide 2008.

No-one is quite sure as to the exact origin of the curious name, the most popular theory is that the then ale-keeper passed information to the Crown during the Jacobite uprisings of 1715 and 1745 and thus became known as 'The Rat'. This stone building was built in the 18th century but there has been an alehouse on the site for hundreds of years, and the grounds on which it stands are beautiful, the beer garden providing magnificent views. Inside are three warm fireplaces, wooden flooring and various pub paraphernalia decorating the walls including a line of chamber pots!

The bar is welcoming, the little lounge area is very cosy and the warm dining area offers a hint at the locally-sourced, award-winning food that Phil creates.

111

48 LOUGHBROW HOUSE

Hexham, Northumberland NE46 1RS
Tel: 01434 603351   Fax: 01434 609774
website: www.loughbrowhouse.co.uk

Loughbrow House is a distinguished 18th century country mansion in a beautiful, tranquil setting high above the River Tyne a mile south of Hexham. A long private drive leads from the B6306 to the house, which stands in nine acres of superb, inspiring gardens. The day rooms and bedrooms are very comfortably furnished in traditional style, with many handsome antiques to enhance the period appeal and well-chosen works of art on the walls. Owner Mrs Clark, who has lived here since 1959, and her staff create a relaxed, civilised ambience in which guests feel that they are part of a private house party rather than Bed & Breakfast guests. The main day room is a spacious and very comfortable drawing room with a lofty ceiling, a grand piano and oil paintings, and there's a second, much smaller lounge that makes a cosy retreat for one or two couples.

The accommodation at Loughbrow House comprises two en suite double-bedded rooms at the front, one with a dressing room that can double as a children's bedroom (children over seven are welcome); and, at the back of the house, an en suite twin-bedded room and two singles that share a bathroom. All the rooms are warm and comfortable, with pleasant views, television and complimentary beverage tray. A hearty breakfast, with home-baked bread and home-made preserves, is served in the dining room, where a three-course candlelit dinner with wine can be ordered with a little notice for parties of four or more.

The garden at Loughbrow House was the inspiration of Mrs Clark and is still her pride and joy, and this sprightly octogenarian is often to be seen pottering in the garden and chatting with the gardeners. The grounds include a woodland garden, two deep herbaceous borders, lawns, shrubs, roses, a bog garden, an arboretum, a small lake from which the house takes its name ('lake on the brow') and a kitchen garden that provides fruit, vegetables, herbs and flowers for the house. The house is a perfect place to take a break from the rush of daily life and a wonderful base for a walking holiday, a golfing holiday (there are three good course nearby), or for exploring the many scenic and historic attractions in the vicinity. Hadrian's Wall is close by, and other places of interest include Hexham Abbey and the site of the Roman town of Corstorpitum.

51 THE HAYES GUEST HOUSE

Newcastle Road, Corbridge,
Northumberland NE45 5LP
Tel: 01434 632010   Fax: 01434 632010
e-mail: camon@surfree.co.uk
website: www.hayes-corbridge.co.uk

Hands-on resident owners Campbell and Monica Matthews offer a choice of guest accommodation an easy stroll from the centre of Corbridge. **The Hayes** is a substantial country house set in seven acres of gardens, woodland and pasture with lovely views southwards over the Tyne valley.

The Bed & Breakfast accommodation comprises two en suite bedrooms, one with twin beds, the other a family room with one double and two single beds. There are also two standard bedrooms – one with a double and two single beds, and a single room. These two rooms have the use of a private bathroom. All the rooms have tea/coffee making facilities, TV, clock-radio and hairdryer, and breakfast is served in a dining room that also serves as a TV lounge. Children are welcome, and the B&B terms include reductions for children and for stays of three or more nights.

The self-catering accommodation, sleeping 4 or 5) is in Stable and Bothy Cottages, which form part of a small courtyard and were originally the stables. The bedrooms – a double and a single – are located on the first floor. On the ground floor, Stable and Bothy each have well-equipped kitchens, dining and lounge areas, and a sofa bed (Bothy) and an extra bed

in an annexe (Stable) provide sleeping space for a fifth guest. Both have fitted carpets, full gas central heating, electric cooker, microwave, dishwasher, fridge, washing machine, TV, radio-clock, hairdryer and pine dining furniture. Booking run from Saturday to Saturday except for out-of-season short breaks, and guests are welcome to bring their pets. Coarse and fly fishing is available on the River Tyne.

Corbridge, once the capital of the ancient Kingdom of Northumbria, is a lively little market town that's well worth taking time to explore. The Church of St Andrew retains many Saxon features, and a complete Roman arch is incorporated into the tower wall. Corbridge is the site of the annual Northumberland County Show. It is also an excellent base for discovering the amazing abundance of history in the vicinity. The substantial remains of the Roman military town of Corstorpitum are close by, while that attractions of nearby Hexham range from the abbey, church and museum to the arts centre and the National Hunt racecourse.

50 THE DYVELS INN

Station Road, Corbridge,
Northumberland NE45 5AY
Tel: 01434 633633
e-mail: thedyvelsinn@googlemail.com
website: www.dyvelsinn.co.uk

In their welcoming stone inn David and Gemma Harding have created a great atmosphere in which to enjoy a good variety of drinks and excellent food at  very reasonable prices. The diverse menu at the **Dyvels Inn**, served lunchtime and evening Monday to Saturday and from 12 to 4 on Sunday for traditional roasts, ranges from sandwiches and toasties to hearty favourites like sausages with mustard mash. The inn is open from noon to 11 every day, and when the sun shines the seats on the terrace are a pleasant alternative to the large, comfortable bar. The inn has a good local following, and its three en suite bedrooms offer a quiet base for tourists, walkers and cyclists.

52 GREENCARTS

Greencarts Farm, Neal, Humshaugh,
nr Hexham, Northumberland NE46 4BW
Tel: 01434 681320
e-mail: Sandra@greencarts.co.uk
website: www.greencarts.co.uk

A variety of accommodation caters for all at **Greencarts**, which lies in stunning countryside right by Hadrian's Wall. The Maughan family's 14th century farmhouse has two double and one twin bedroom, all en suite, for B&B guests, whose day starts with a hearty Northumbrian breakfast (evening meals with notice).  The bunk barn provides excellent bunkhouse accommodation for up to 8 guests, with good kitchen and washroom facilities and a drying/boot room. A camping barn offers more basic dormitory-style sleeping in four bunk beds, and the campsite has space for 30 pitches, with washrooms and toilets that can also be used by camping barn guests.

53 HALLBARNS B&B

Hallbarns, Simonburn, nr Hexham,
Northumberland NE48 3AQ
Tel: 01434 681419
e-mail: enquiries@hallbarns-
simonburn.co.uk
website: www.hallbarns-simonburn.co.uk

Dick and Margaret have a genuinely warm greeting for guests at **Hallbarns B&B**, a traditional stone farmhouse on a working farm at Simonburn, just north of Hadrian's Wall. The setting is both beautiful and peaceful, with views of Chipchase Castle across the valley of the North Tyne, a river famous for its salmon fishing.

Recently refurbished to a very high standard and awarded 4 Stars by Visit Britain, the three excellent bedrooms – a twin with shower en suite, a twin with private bath and shower and a family room with a double bed, a single bed with a roll-out bed beneath and en suite bath and shower. A real log fire keeps things cosy in the sitting room, and the house has a patio and lawn for sitting out or strolling when the sun shines.

A traditional farmhouse breakfast cooked on the Aga is the perfect way to start a day exploring the lovely surroundings, and packed lunches and evening meals can be provided with a little notice. Facilities at Hallbarns include stabling for up to four horses: this is a wonderful area for riding and there are meetings for Trial Hunting every day except Friday and Sunday. There are also excellent facilities for walking, cycling, birdwatching and of course sightseeing – Hadrian's Wall is one of the country's most visited attractions. Hallbarns is open all year round for short or long days.

54 READING ROOMS

2 Church Street, Haydon Bridge,
nr Hexham, Northumberland NE47 6JQ
Tel: 01434 688 802
e-mail: thereadingrooms@aol.com
website:
www.thereadingroomshaydonbridge.co.uk

Originally built in 1850 as the village **Reading Rooms**, this was a venue for gentlemen to read the newspapers and the Bible. 150 years on, Gill Valentine has turned the premises into a gorgeous 4 star B & B, which is enjoying a fast growing reputation both at home and abroad for comfort and relaxation. Haydon Bridge, where the Reading Rooms can be found, lies on the East/West border of North England along the main route North in the heart of many local attractions such as the Lake District and heritage sites like Hadrian's Wall. The village, which dates from the 12th century, includes a co-op, a pub and a restaurant for evening amusement and the B & B is in beautiful spot on the Tyne river.

Gill has strived to create a 'home away from home' and caters for many interests, providing services like easy parking, a secure shed for cycles, a drying room for walking boots and even a packed lunch for the day ahead. The three en-suite rooms are all large, airy and furnished to a high standard, after a relaxing night's sleep, guests are treated to a large breakfast, all made using locally sourced produce.

55 GRINDON CARTSHED

Grindon Farm, Haydon Bridge, Hexham,
Northumbria NE47 6NQ
Tel: 01434 684273
website: www.grindon-cartshed.co.uk

Northumberland is renowned for its friendly people, astounding scenery and Hadrian's Roman Wall. If you don't know Northumberland you have a treat in store. **Grindon Cartshed** offers you the freedom to enjoy the pleasures of Northumberland throughout the year while living comfortably in the pleasant family atmosphere of a cosy farm conversion adapted especially to receive holiday makers, both bed and breakfast and self-catering.

Delightful hosts, Dave and Jackie Armstrong extend a warm welcome to all their guests at their farm, which is a 600 hundred-acre hill farm nestled within the Hadrian's Wall corridor. A notable attraction is the small flock of coloured Ryeland sheep. The dramatic country has inspired Dave and Jackie to protect their natural heritage. They farm in an

environmentally sensitive way and are passionate about using and supplying local produce. The business supplies meats from the local butchers; they promote local beer and supply local eggs and other produce from nearby farms. They also provide locally produced crafts such as soaps, greetings cards and textile products. While away the time relaxing in the licensed dining room while enjoying a delicious evening meal. Do not stop there, however. Grindon Cartshed is surrounded by some of the most beautiful countryside you could wish to see.

56 VINDOLANDA AND ROMAN ARMY MUSEUM

The Vindolanda Trust, Chesterholme
Museum, Bardon Mill,
Hexham, Northumberland NE47 7JN
Vindolanda Tel: 01434 344277
Roman Army Museum Tel: 016977 47485
e-mail: info@vindolanda.com
website: www.vindolanda.com

Vindolanda was once a Roman frontier military and civilain site. Substantial remains are visible and on display are rare and fascinating objects from the past, including Roman boots and shoes, jewellery, tools, locks and textiles. Special photographs

of rare ink on wood letters, written nearly 2000 years ago, are also on show. The Open Air Museum has full sized replicas of a Roman Temple, a Roman shop, a Roman house, as well as a Northumbrian croft, all set in relaxing gardens.

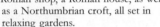

The **Roman Army Museum** is located next to the superb Walltown Crags section of Hadrian's Wall and gives a fascinating insight into life as a Roman soldier, garrisoned along the forts and milecastles of the Wall. Here you can find out about the weapons, uniforms, pay, training and off duty activities. The Museum has reconstructions, life sized figures, Roman objects, films and much more.

Both sites are open daily form 10am and have good facilities. Both have coffee shops serving light snacks and a gift shop selling a range of gifts and souvenirs. Both have toilets, picnic sites, free parking and disabled access.

57 THE GOLDEN LION

The Market Place, Allendale,
Hexham, Northumberland NE46 9BD
Tel: 01434 683 225

A fine old traditional hostelry, **The Golden Lion** has been dispensing hospitality since 1660. The interior is full of charm and character, especially when the open fires are blazing away. Mine hosts at this friendly and lively tavern are Gloria and Ian Armstrong who have been in the business for some 20 years. Real ale lovers will be delighted to find no fewer than 5 different brews on tap including Black Sheep and local ales from Allendale and Wylam breweries.

The inn is well-known for its appetising home-cooked food with old favourites such as Steak & Ale Pie and Fisherman's Pie featuring on the menu along with dishes such as Chicken & Leek Pie and vegetarian choices. The inn is very much the social centre of Allendale, regularly used by organisations such as the Allendale Lions and the dale singers. It also has its own pool teams. The inn welcomes dogs and there's free parking outside the pub.

58 THE ALLENDALE INN

Market Place, Allendale,
Northumberland NE47 9BJ
Tel: 01434 683246
e-mail: whobday@bigfoot.com

A warm welcome and a friendly, relaxed atmosphere await visitors to the **Allendale Inn**, which stands on the market place of the town that lies exactly halfway between Beachy Head in Sussex and Cape Wrath in the Scottish Highlands. Surrounded by the beautiful

Northumbrian countryside, it attracts walkers, tourists and sightseers as well as locals, and in the low-ceilinged beamed bar with its feature fireplace they all get together with host Bill Hobday to enjoy a drink and a value-for-money snack or meal using fresh local produce – and perhaps a game of darts. The bar is open from 10am to 11pm (Friday and Saturday to midnight, Sunday 11 to 11).

59 ALLENDALE TEA ROOMS

Market Place, Allendale, nr Hexham,
Northumberland NE47 9BD
Tel: 01434 683575
e-mail: susanbayfield@hotmail.co.uk
website: www.allendaletearooms.co.uk

On the market place of the town from which it takes its name, the **Allendale Tea Rooms** occupy a Grade II listed mid-Victorian stone building with a slate roof, sash windows and hanging baskets. Terry and Susan changed careers and surroundings when they took over here in May 2008, and the combination of customer service, a friendly, relaxed atmosphere and value for money attracts a wide cross-section of customers, from locals and shoppers to walkers, cyclists, motorists, tourists and day trippers. The licensed tea rooms are open from 10 to 5 Tuesday to Saturday, from 11 to 5 on Sunday and on Mondays on Bank Holidays and in high season for an excellent selection of traditional, home-cooked food, from breakfasts to light lunches, Sunday roasts, cakes and pastries.

Above the tea rooms are two well-kept

bedrooms for Bed & Breakfast guests. The double and twin rooms provide a comfortable, civilised base for touring the North Pennines and discovering the local sights. A hearty breakfast gets the day off to a fine start, and an evening meal is available by arrangement.

**Westbourne House, Main Street,
Haltwhistle, Northumberland NE49 0AZ
Tel: 01434 321 780**

Haltwhistle is one of two towns in Great Britain that can claim to be geographically in the centre of the Island and it is here on the main street that the **Pillar Box Café** can be found. The name is given for the fact that the café stands next to the Post Office.

The town of Haltwhistle is almost on the border of the North East and West, in a prime position to visit Hadrian's Wall, the most complete section of which is just 10 minutes away. The small frontage of the cafe holds pretty hanging baskets and this sets the scene for the simple, homely and relaxing interior, which is more spacious than one would think. The décor and linen tablecloths, along with the friendly service provide an excellent eating experience.

The extensive menu offers something for everybody, from hearty full English breakfasts and home-made pies to panini and toasted sandwiches for a light snack. The café is open from Monday to Saturday with a half day on Wednesday and is open from 9am daily. There are full disabled facilities and children are very welcome, with a children's menu available.

**West Woodburn, Kielder,
Northumberland NE48 2RX
Tel: 01434 270218
website: www.bayhorseinn.org**

The **Bay Horse Inn** is a late-18th century mellow sandstone hostelry standing in the heart of the Cheviot Hills, by a stone bridge on the main A68. Hilda Wright, who was first associated with the inn 20 years ago, is an admirable host and her immaculate inn is a delightful place to pause for a drink, to relax over a leisurely meal or to enjoy a break in a picturesque setting.

Food is very much the star here, with prime local produce taking centre stage for the home-cooked dishes on the wide-ranging menus. Among the perennial favourites are beer-battered haddock, lasagne, chilli con carne, mince with dumplings, lamb chops, chicken tikka masala and specials featuring seafood caught off the nearby Northumberland coast. The five cottage-style guest bedrooms, each with its own individual character, have en suite facilities, TV and hot drinks tray; they provide an ideal base for tourists, cyclists and walkers – the Pennine Way passes close by. The Bay Horse hosts occasional live music nights and a quiz every other Thursday.

Wark-onTyne,
Northumberland, NE48 3NT
Tel: 01434 230203

Early in the 13th century there was already a chapel, a park, and a mill at Chipchase.

The first owner of **Chipchase Castle** on record is Sir Per de Insula living about the middle of the thirteenth century. Later through marriage the Heron family retained possession of Chipchase for over 350 years.

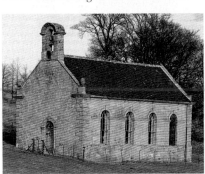

The Herons built and lived in a strong stone tower until a new Manor house was built in the 17th century. New owners in the 18th century considerably altered the exterior of this building, and the new chapel that was built in the 18th century is still in use today.

The house opens from June 1st to June 28th between 2pm and 5pm. Castle Gardens and the Nursery Garden are open from Easter to 31st July, Thursday to Sunday and Bank Holiday Mondays 10am to 5pm.

There are three acres of gardens that surround the medieval/Jacobean castle and walled nursery garden that specialise in unusual hardy plants.

HIDDEN PLACES GUIDES

Explore Britain and Ireland with *Hidden Places* guides - a fascinating series of national and local travel guides.

Packed with easy to read information on hundreds of places of interest as well as places to stay, eat and drink.

Available from both high street and internet booksellers

For more information on the full range of *Hidden Places* guides and other titles published by Travel Publishing visit our website on

www.travelpublishing.co.uk
or ask for our leaflet by phoning
01752 276660 or emailing
info@travelpublishing.co.uk

63 TWENTY SEVEN B&B

27 Castle Drive, Kielder,
Northumberland NE48 IEQ
Tel: 01434 250366
e-mail: tpl@staykielder.co.uk
website: www.staykielder.co.uk

Jill and Terry welcome you **Twenty Seven B&B**, a perfect spot for an overnight stop, a relaxing short break or a longer stay discovering the stunning scenery, dark skies, the wonderful wildlife and the range of outdoor activities of Kielder Water and Forest Park.

The only B&B in tranquil Kielder village, Twenty Seven has three guest bedrooms – a single, a twin and an en suite family room. Amenities include a pleasant garden, secure cycle storage and a laundry room, and packed lunches and evening meals are available with a little notice. The whole house can also be rented on a self-catering basis, with meals by arrangement.

Bellingham Tourist Information
Centre, The Heritage Centre,
Station Yard, Bellingham,
Northumberland NE48 2DG
Tel: 01434 220616
website: www.visitkielder.com

Home to Northern Europe's largest man-made lake, England's largest forest and officially the country's most tranquil spot (Campaign to Protect Rural England), **Kielder Water & Forest Park** is not to be missed.

Nature lovers, water sports enthusiasts, explorers, walkers, cyclists, artists, families … anyone looking to escape, set their own agenda and create new experiences will delight in everything the park has to offer.

The forest itself is one of the main attractions featuring mile upon mile of purpose-built trails including forest walks for all the family and dedicated mountain bike tracks. The Lakeside Way is a unique, multi-user trail suitable for walkers, runners, cyclists, push chair and wheelchair users and horse riders. It encircles Kielder Water stretching for 27 miles (completion Spring 2009).

A haven for wildlife – explorers can expect to encounter deer, otters, badgers, bats and rare breeds of birds. Kielder Water & Forest Park is also home to around 60% of England's native red squirrel population, the last remaining stronghold in the country.

The refurbished hatchery and visitor centre at Kielder Salmon Centre features state of the art facilities for rearing both salmon, and other rare species such as freshwater pearl mussel.

Waterskiing and sailing enthusiasts take to the water all year round and the lake offers a huge challenge to keen trout anglers between March and October. The 'Osprey' ferry is an ideal way to see Kielder Water in comfort.

65 LEAPLISH WATERSIDE PARK

Kielder Water and Forest Park,
Hexham, Northumberland NE48 1BT
Tel: 01434 251000 Fax: 01434 250806
e-mail: kielder.holidays@nwl.co.uk
website: www.nwl.co.uk/kielder

Tucked away on the south side of Kielder Water, in Northumberland, Leaplish Waterside Park houses a number of attractions and accommodation facilities making it an ideal base for visitors and holidaymakers alike.

Leaplish Waterside Park boasts luxury self catering accommodation with seven different types of lodges sleeping between 4 and 6 people and are rated as either 4 or 5 star accommodation from the English tourist board. The lodges are furnished to high standards and all have verandas to make the most of the superb views over the surrounding countryside.

The facilities and attractions at Leaplish Waterside Park make it an idyllic place for all to enjoy at your own pace, you can:

- Soothe your senses with a sauna and a swim in the indoor heated pool

- Unwind by the lakeside in the peaceful Boat Inn restaurant and bar

- Board the Osprey ferry and cross the lake as you experience the breathtaking views of Kielder Water

- Hire a pleasure boat and explore the hidden coves and bays

- Discover the huge variety of wildlife including red squirrel, otters, deer and many rare species

- Take a stroll along the scenic lakeside way and discover the unique art and architecture

- Visit the Bird of Prey Centre and get up close and personal with the world's most captivating birds of prey

- Let your children create their own adventures as they enjoy a range of attractions including the play garden, mapping mini golf and wildlife

The lodges are a perfect accompaniment to your visit to whether you have had a hectic day out and about, or have enjoyed just relaxing, then the very comfortable spacious lodges will suit your needs.

Leaplish Waterside Park is also a great base to explore England's largest World Heritage Site, Hadrian's Wall, the market towns, castles and coastlines of Northumberland along with Cumbria and the Scottish Borders.

66 GO FISHING WITH NORTHUMBRIAN WATER

Tel: 0870 240 3549
website: www.nwl.co.uk/gofishing

The lakes are set in some of the region's most spectacular countryside helping to make a visit to one of the waters a great day out for all the family. You can enjoy fishing, walking, take a picnic or just relax in some of England's most beautiful surroundings. The main sites have well stocked shops where you can get a range of fishing and leisure goods along with snacks and drinks for your great day out. Most venues are suitable for disabled anglers and visitors.

1. Fontburn Reservoir

Tel: Shop and Rangers 01669 621368

Fontburn offers top class fishing for the fly and bait angler alike. Add to this a tremendous setting amongst the Simonside Hills and the result is a perfect venue for trout anglers. For non-anglers there is a pleasant walk along the south shoreline and a spacious picnic area. Fontburn is just off the A696 close to Rothbury (Satnav NE61 4PL).

2. Kielder Water & Forest Park

Tel: Bookings and information 01434 251000

If you like big water boat and bank fishing then Kielder Water and Forest Park is the place to be, with a fleet of fully equipped motor boats the huge lake offers exhilarating fishing for both the enthusiast and competitive angler. Wheelie boats are available for the disabled angler. For short breaks there are luxury lodges where you and your guests can fish free (excluding boat hire) for the duration of the stay. It is situated 12 miles west of Bellingham, easily accessible from the A69 at Hexham (Satnav NE48 1BT).

3. Whittle Dene Lakes

Tel: Shop and rangers 01669 621368

Located right on the old military road near Harlow Hill just off the B6318, Whittle Dene has a choice of four lakes each containing a good head of wild species such as roach, perch, dace and gudgeon. Skimmers were introduced in 2006 making the Lower Lake a prime match and pleasure fishing venue (Satnav NE15 0QA)

4. Derwent Reservoir

Tel: Shop and Rangers 01207 255250

Derwent Reservoir is the place to go if you like wide open spaces and the chance to catch superb specimen fish. New anglers can take advantage of fishing lessons held at Derwent throughout the season. It is just off the A68, four miles west of Castleside (Satnav DH8 9TT).

5, 8 and 9. Wild Brown Trout

Tel: Shop and rangers 01833 641121 – based at Grassholme

For the real enthusiast why not get trult get away from it all by visitng one of the prime wild brown trout fisheries. Each is situated in the remote upper reaches of Teesdale or one of its tributary valleys; Cow Green, Selset and Balderhead all offer a unique blend of wilderness and superb wild brownies, who ounce for ounce, outfight the rainbow every time.

6. Grassholme Reservoir

Tel: Shop and Rangers 01833 641121

Teesdales's most popular fishery, Grassholme has a picture postcard setting typical of the Pennine Dales. The visitor centre has a hands-on exhibition for children and there is a circular footpath around the lake giving magnificent views across the water. It is just off the B6277 between Barnard Castle and Mickleton (Satnav DL12 0PW).

7. Hury Reservoir

Tel: Shop and rangers 01833 641121

After a couple of seasons as a coarse fishery, Hury is back as Teesdale's premier fly only water. It is stocked weekly with grown on fish and is a must for the traditional fly fishing enthusiast. The lake can be reached from either Romaldkirk or Cotherstone off the B6277 (Satnav DL12 9UP).

10. Scaling Reservoir

Tel: Shop and rangers 01287 644032

Scaling has a very pleasant circular walk, a section of which is wheelchair accessible, plus several very lovely picnic areas offering wonderful views across the lake. It holds specimen pike to 30lbs and is good for both fly and bait fishing. It is located between Guisborough and Whitby on the A171 (Satnav TS13 4TR).

Kielder Water Bird of Prey Centre
Leaplish Waterside Park,
Kielder, Northumberland, NE48 1AX
Tel: 01434 250500
website: www.discoverit.co.uk/falconry

The Birds of Prey Centre is located within the magnificent forest lakeside surroundings of Kielder Water at Leaplish Waterside Park. The centre contains one of the largest and most fascinating collections of Birds of prey in the north of England.

At the birds of Prey Centre you will discover a vast variety of species and find out about their essential role within the ecology of the natural world.

Experience the thrills and excitement of handling some of these beautiful and extraordinary birds.

Learn about the valuble work of the Keilder Water Bird of Prey Centre's Captive Breeding Programme, which has been established to further the awareness of conservation, propagation and rehabilitation of Birds of Prey.

Falconry is one of the oldest and most aristocratic sports and for many centuries has been regarded as the sport of Kings with the falcon as a symbol of high birth and society. Hunting with birds of prey or raptors was practiced in China as long ago as 2000 B.C.

Later, falconry developed as a sport practiced by members of Royal households, with each rank of nobility permitted to use only certain species of birds.

Today, falconry is widely pursued in most European countries and in the United States, although the Arabian peninsula remains the area where the sport is held in highest regard.

As well as being able to get close to birds of prey there are daily demonstrations (weather permitting). This is a fantastic opportunity to see birds of prey in actions. Watch a Peregrine Falcon stoop down from the skies at over 100 mph, see the grace and speed of a Russian eagle.

The Birds of Prey Centre offers visitors an opportunity to share in a direct 'hands on' experience during which they will meet all the northern region's indigenous Owls as well as birds of prey from around the world – all within a professionally supervised environment.

**High Street, Rothbury,
Northumberland NE65 7TE
Tel: 01669 621337**

Helen Renton and her family continue to win friends at the **Elm Tree Coffee Shop**. Since arriving here they have built up a fine reputation for quality and value for money in their handsome former Victorian town house, which looks down Rothbury's High Street from its elevated position.

The two rooms offer a delightfully unfussy and relaxed ambience in which to enjoy good honest home cooking. Counter service provides excellent teas and coffees and hot and cold drinks to accompany scones, cakes, filled rolls, toasties, jacket potatoes with interesting toppings, savoury pies and daily specials. Everything is fresh and wholesome, freshly made each day on the premises

and pleasantly light on the pocket. Helen, her family and their staff are always friendly, willing and ready to help, making it a pleasure to return time and again to the Elm Tree, which is open from 10 to 5 (till 4 off season) seven days a week.

It's fully accessible (including the toilets) to wheel chairs. Some free parking is usually available directly outside the coffee shop, and the large village car park by the river is just two minutes' walk away.

The Elm Tree would make a lovely place for a small party or get together: groups are welcome – phone to arrange – and a private room is available. Rothbury is a pleasant little town and a perfect base for exploring the lovely valley of the River Coquet. Once the setting of an important livestock market, it's now an attractive resort for walkers and fisherman. The former Saxon parish church is well worth a visit, and just outside town is the National Trust's Cragside, the first house in the world to be lit by hydroelectricity. After a shopping expedition, a walk round the town or a breath of fresh air in the surrounding countryside there are few more agreeable places to take a break than the Elm Tree Coffee Shop.

Main Street, Thropton,
Northumberland NE65 7LR
Tel: 01669 620262
website: www.threewheatheads.com

The **Three Wheat Heads** enjoys a serene, picturesque setting in the heart of Coquetdale, 2 miles from Rothbury and 12 miles from Alnwick. This charming village hostelry, built of local stone in the 17th century, has been beautifully restored to preserve all the finest period features. The carpeted lounge bar, warmed by a real coal fire in the cooler months, is a delightful spot to enjoy a drink and make or meet friends, and when the sun shines the superb beer garden, with views across to the Simonside Hills, is the place to be.

Well-kept ales from Marstons and Theakstons breweries are among the favourite thirst-quenchers, and the landlords keep an excellent cellar to complement the food for which the pub is renowned. In the elegant surroundings of the restaurant, with antiques and well-chosen pictures, patrons can enjoy a fine variety of dishes cooked to order. The chefs set great store by the finest local produce, including Aberdeen Angus beef from nearby farms and salmon from the neighbouring Coquet river. Restaurant and bar menus offer plenty of choice of meat, game, fish and vegetarian dishes. The bar is open from 12 to 11 seven days a week for drinks; food times are 12 to 2.30 and 6 to 9 Monday to Friday, 12 to 9 Saturday and Sunday.

As well as being the heartbeat of the local community and an acclaimed dining destination, the Three Wheat Heads is also a perfect choice for a break in quiet, beautiful surroundings. Single and double rooms, all with en suite facilities, are decorated and furnished to impressively high standards, and all have televisions, beverage trays and the thoughtful little extras that make guests feel instantly at home. Room service is available on request, and guests start the day with a generous, freshly cooked breakfast.

The village of Thropton lies two miles west of Rothbury near the junction of the Coquet river and Wreigh Burn. From the A1 just north of the Morpeth by-pass, take the A697 to the Weldon Bridge exit then the B6344 through Rothbury. Thropton is two miles further on, and the Three Wheat Haeds stands in the centre of the village next to the United Reform Church building. The area offers great walking and fishing opportunities and local places of interest include Brinkburn Priory and the National Trust's Cragside.

70 THE ANCHOR INN

2 Cheviot Street, Wooler,
Northumberland NE71 6LN
Tel: 01668 281412
e-mail: the.anchor.inn@btconnect.com
website: www.anchorinnwooler.co.uk

Wooler is a small town set in great walking country at the northern end of the Cheviots. One of the most pleasant and popular meeting places in the town is the **Anchor Inn**, where landlady Carol Johnson guarantees the warmest of welcomes for one and all. Sal, who does the cooking, is equally friendly and entertaining, and their friendly chat and sense of humour create a lovely, lively atmosphere. The whole place has been smartly refurbished, from the bar/lounge to the dining room, the pool room, the terrace and the beer garden.

Black Sheep is the resident real ale served in the bars, which are open all day, every day. Sal attracts locals, walkers, cyclists, bikers, motorists and holidaymakers with her generous helpings of value-for-money food, which runs from light snacks and sandwiches to pub classics like burgers, scampi, sausages & mash, gammon and beef steaks, curries, lamb shanks and steak & ale pie. Her rhubarb & ginger chutney is the prefect accompaniment to meat and cheese, and her sticky toffee pudding and ginger pudding are legends in the region.

The Anchor's three well-equipped en suite guest bedrooms provide an ideal base for discovering the scenic and historic delights of the countryside, the coast and the border country.

71 THE WHEATSHEAF HOTEL

10 Market Place, Wooler,
Northumberland NE71 6LH
Tel: 01668 281434
e-mail: wheatsheafwooler@btinternet.com

On the market place in the pleasant little town of Wooler, the **Wheatsheaf Hotel** is a friendly, comfortable base for touring the Cheviots, the Northumberland National Park and the coast. The handsome mid-Victorian hotel is run by David and Wendy, who brought many years' experience in running hotels and inns when they took over here. They share the hosting and the cooking, and David's mother is also very much part of the team, making sure that everything is spick and span. The hotel is a popular choice with tourists, walkers, cyclists and golfers – David is a keen golfer and knows all about the local courses (there are 15 within a 30-minute drive!).

The accommodation comprises three doubles and a family room, all with en suite facilities, TV with Freeview

and a hot drinks tray, and the day starts with a substantial cooked breakfast. The Wheatsheaf is also a very agreeable local meeting place for a drink or a meal. The bar is open from noon to midnight (to 1am Friday and Saturday) for a good choice of drinks, and food catering for all tastes and appetites is served in the bar or separate dining room every lunchtime and evening. The public rooms and toilets area are accessible to wheelchairs, but not the bedrooms.

72 MOJO'S CAFÉ

48 High Street, Wooler,
Northumberland NE71 6BG
Tel: 07880 811516

Mojo's is a popular café-bistro on the main street of Wooler, with plenty of nearby parking. Jo-Anne Hardy, who took over this delightful place in July 2007 and gave it its new name, is young, friendly and hard-working, with equally affable staff who always put the customer first. Locals, families, walkers, cyclists and tourists are all equally welcome, and fun and banter are guaranteed in a lively, relaxed atmosphere.

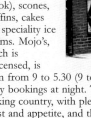

In the neat, bright room, with lightwood tables and wicker chairs, customers can enjoy a fine range of snacks and meals both sweet and savoury. The choice runs from hot breakfast rolls, stotties, toasties and panini to jacket potatoes, pasta dishes, salads, all-day breakfasts, Sunday roasts (best to book), scones,

muffins, cakes and speciality ice creams. Mojo's, which is unlicensed, is open from 9 to 5.30 (9 to 4 in winter) and we also do private party bookings at night. The area round Wooler is great walking country, with plenty of opportunities for building up a thirst and appetite, and there's no more agreeable spot for taking care of them than Mojo's.

73 THE RED LION INN

Main Road, Milfield, nr Wooler,
Northumberland NE71 6JD
Tel: 01668 216224
e-mail: iaindburn@fsmail.net
website: www.redlioninn-milfield.co.uk

The **Red Lion Inn** is a classic windstone building dating from the middle of the 18th century. Once providing rest and refreshment for sheep-drovers, and later a stop for passengers and horses on the London-Edinburgh coaching run, it is now a cosy, welcoming Inn with outstanding hosts in Iain and Clare Burn. They extend a traditional welcome and unbeatable hospitality to all who pass through the door, from locals to walkers, cyclists, anglers (there are several good fishing rivers nearby) and gliders.

The bar is a great place for enjoying a glass or two of real ale (Scottish & Newcastle brews and regularly changing guests) with great conversation. Iain prides himself on the quality and value for money his menu provides. He uses fresh seasonal ingredients from the region whenever possible for his wholesome dishes, which include daily fish specials and a signature dish of honey-roast belly pork with bubble & squeak

mash. The inn's three roomy en suite bedrooms (a double, a triple and a family room) provide an ideal base for pausing on a journey to Scotland or for exploring the rich history and beautiful scenery of the region.

The Northumberland National Park is just down the road, the coast and Holy island are an easy drive away and other attractions in the vicinity include the Battlefield of Flodden and the estate villages of Ford and Etal. The village of Milfield, which grew around the inn, lies on the A697 between Wooler and Cornhill-on-Tweed.

74 THE BLACK BULL

Etal Village, Cornhill-on-Tweed,
Northumberland TD12 4TL
Tel: 01890 820200

As pretty as a picture, the **Black Bull** is a whitewashed, thatch-roofed village inn with a history going back eight centuries. This charming exterior, adorned by hanging baskets in spring and summer, is matched by the interior with its beams, thick walls and a unique decorative feature of hundreds of witch dolls from all round the world.

Resident owner Karen Hunter has built up a strong and loyal local following with her warm welcome and genuine hospitality, and her chef Stephen Percival enjoys an ever-widening reputation with his honest, generous cooking based on prime Northumberland produce (his pies are definitely not to be missed). As well as being a great place for a drink and a meal, the Black Bull is also the social hub of the local community, with regular events throughout the year, from barbecues in the beer garden to Morris dancers, raft races and Hallowe'en celebrations. The pub is closed on Tuesday in winter.

In the same ownership as the Black Bull is **The Witchery**, down the A697 in the village of Thropton, near Rothbury, close to the River Coquet on the edge of the Northumberland National Park. This mid-terrace cottage for four provides an idyllic self-catering base for exploring the unspoilt countryside and discovering the wealth of local history.

75 LADY WATERFORD HALL

Ford & Etal Estates, Ford, Cornhill on
Tweed, Northumberland TD15 2QA
Tel: 01890 820338
e-mail: tourisim@ford-and-etal.com
website: www.ford-and-etal.co.uk

Containing unique Northumbrian artworks by Lady Waterford and other artefacts from her time, this wonderful building should not be missed. **Lady Waterford Hall**, a striking building, served as the village school until 1957, and is now the Village Hall. Recognised as one of the most interesting and gifted artists of the

Victoria era, Lady Waterford spent the years between 1862 and 1883 decorating the walls with life size paintings. They depict children from the school, and people who lived in and around Ford, as well as characters from well-known biblical scenes.

78 BELSAY HALL CASTLE AND GARDENS

Belsay, near Ponteland,
Northumberland NE20 ODX
Tel: 01661 881297 Fax: 01661 881043
website: www.english-heritage.org.uk

Why not indulge yourself by visiting one of the best English Heritage properties in the area – **Belsay Hall Castle and Gardens**. The hall was built for Sir Charles Monck on an estate that already had a castle and Jacobean mansion, and they all stand in 30 beautiful acres of landscaped gardens. There's a

magnolia garden, terraces, rhododendrons, a winter garden and croquet lawn, and a quarry garden. The whole estate has been listed as Grade 1 in the Register of gardens. In addition there's free parking, a tearoom (summer only) and various small exhibitions.

76 THE TOWER

5 Oldgate, Morpeth,
Nothumberland NE61 1PY
Tel: 01670 514666

Light, bright and modern, **The Tower** is a popular café, bistro and grill by the market square in Morpeth. It takes its name from the neighbouring stone clock tower, which has been a landmark in the town for many centuries.

Owner Rebecca Peddis, who refitted and relaunched the café in November 2007, has quickly made it a favourite eating place in the town, open from 9am to 8.30 (last orders) Monday to Saturday. The light bite menu, available from opening time until 5 o'clock, offers scones, muffins, omelettes, brunch (including a vegetarian option) and ciabattas/wraps with a wide variety of fillings. The main menu, which comes on stream at 11.30, tempts with an impressive selection of dishes to suit all tastes and appetites. Starters like garlic prawns or dolcelatte-stuffed mushrooms

might precede a beef or chicken burger (choose from a dozen toppings), pizza, pasta, chicken schnitzel, kleftiko or grilled tuna steak with a sweet chilli salsa. The drinks list is equally diverse, from soft drinks, tea and coffee to beers, spirits and wines available by 125 and 250cl glass, 500cl carafe and 750cl bottle.

The Tower is popular with locals and tourists alike and everyone loves the happy hour, which operates between 5 and 7, with bargains on drinks and the pizza/pasta menu. There's ramp access to the café and there are disabled facilities in the ladies loo.

77 THE DYKE NEUK INN

Meldon, Morpeth,
Northumberland NE61 3SL
Tel: 01670 772 662
e-mail: mooreyspot@aol.com

The **Dyke Neuk Inn** is a stone built bed and breakfast offering fantastic views of Northumberland, owned since July 2007 by the welcoming Forster family, this inn is a delightful place to eat, drink and sleep. With the nearby Bolam Lake and Wallington Hall attracting visitors from all over the country, the Dyke Neuk Inn is used to catering for all types of guests.

Inside the décor is of a quality feel, with slate floors and stone walls in the pub and restaurant. Upstairs, the 4 star B and B has been recently refurbished to a very high standard and the 4 en-suite rooms are all very comfortable. The restaurant provides home cooked traditional dishes, such as the popular Steak and Kidney pie. The bar is well stocked and

carries two real ales from the local Wylam Brewery, which was awarded the

prestigious Champion Beer in the 2001 CAMRA Newcastle Beer Festival. There is also a games area, which plays host to quiz nights, special offer nights and occasional live music. The pub is open daily from 12pm till late with food available Tues to Sat, 7pm – 9pm and 12pm – 9pm on Sundays.

Longhirst, Morpeth,
Northumberland NE61 3LP
Tel: 01670 794530 Fax: 01670 791330
e-mail: info@micklewoodpark.co.uk
website: www.micklewoodpark.co.uk

Micklewood Park offers an affordable, safe and secure holiday base for families, friends and special interest groups. Thirty-six self-catering homes are located in the 75-acre grounds of Longhirst Hall, a short distance north of Morpeth. They have up to five bedrooms, providing outstanding accommodation for between four and ten people. All are practically appointed and comfortably furnished, with a large kitchen/dining area, lounge (TV with Freeview and DVD player), bath and

shower room. The rental includes all heating and electricity, linen and towels and a welcome pack of kitchen essentials. A delivery service from the local grocer is available (a list is sent out with confirmation of booking) and the homes share a barbecue and picnic area for eating out of doors. A number of the units are adapted for disabled guests. For larger groups two or more holiday homes can be reserved together. Pets are welcome, but dogs should be kept on a leash when in the grounds. The usual rental is on a weekly or longer basis, but short breaks (3 days minimum) are offered, so Micklewood Park is a great place for a weekend break as well as a longer stay.

The Park is well placed for exploring Northumberland's beautiful coastline and countryside, but there's plenty to do without ever leaving the site. Extensive leisure and sporting facilities include a golf course, tennis courts and cricket, football and hockey pitches. It's a superb place for children, who receive a backpack full of goodies on arrival and are encouraged to take an active interest in nature by joining Micklewood's Secret Squirrel Club. An outdoor adventure area has a climbing frame and rope swings, goal posts and basketball hoops. And if the sun stops shining, the scene can shift to The Den, with table tennis and football, a pool table, air hockey and a host of other games.

The central reception and meeting place is The Hub, the information point where trips, visits and activities can be arranged – anything from cycling and sailing to a hot-air balloon flight. The facilities of Longhirst Hall are available to all guests, notably fine dining in the stylish Boyson Restaurant. A half-board option provides a full breakfast and three-course evening meal.

The Park is located a short drive from the A1, 2 miles north of Morpeth– look for signs to Hebron and Longhirst Hall.

80 NEVIN'S NIBBLES

4 Bridge Street, Newbiggin-by-the-Sea,
Northumberland NE64 6EG
Tel: 01670 816271
e-mail: colin.nevin@virgin.net

Colin and Jackie Nevin own and run **Nevin's Nibbles**, a bright modern café/ restaurant by the bandstand (a popular venue for open-air events) and the much acclaimed statue of a couple looking out to sea. Jackie has been in catering all her working life and really loves cooking, and in an informal, relaxed ambience that epitomises Newbiggin's confident new air, locals, walkers, cyclists and tourists return again and again to enjoy her value-for-money home cooking.

A full menu of snacks and meals is served from 8am to 8pm (Sunday from 10) in summer and from 8am to 5pm out of season. The choice runs from a light sweet or savoury snack to a hearty all-day breakfast, and children can choose from their own menu.

The stylish 1930s building, which previously housed Bertorelli's, stands right by the promenade a short walk from a much-visited Heritage Site. The café has access for wheelchairs and mobility scooters, and full disabled toilet facilities were introduced in July 2008. The fishing village and small resort of Newbiggin is well worth taking time for a stroll, and among the attractions are that statue, St Bartholomew's Church and the oldest operational lifeboat house in Britain.

81 HAGG FARMHOUSE B&B

Ellington, Morpeth,
Northumberland NE61 5JW
Tel: 01670 860514
e-mail: Cheryl.smith@haggfarmhouse.com
website: www.haggfarmhouse.com

Cheryl Smith puts out the welcome mat for tourists, cyclists, motorcyclists, groups of friends and families with children to **Hagg Farmhouse**, which stands near the village of Ellington, on the A1068 about 7 miles northeast of Morpeth, 8 miles from the A1 and just 2 miles from the coast.

The Bed & Breakfast accommodation, smartly refurbished in 2006, comprises three comfortable, well-furnished rooms – a single, a double and a family room with space for two adults and up to three children. One room has en suite facilities and all have TV, hot drinks tray and views of the beautiful Northumberland countryside. The farmhouse has a guest lounge with TV, DVD and internet access, a large rear garden and ample car parking space. Hagg Farmhouse is ideally situated for many of the county's major attractions.

There are facilities for walking, picnicking, sailing, canoeing, windsurfing and birdwatching at Druridge Country Park, which is set just behind the sand dunes and grasslands of Druridge Bay. There are also outdoor activities to enjoy at Wansbeck Riverside Park, and other places well worth a visit include the little fishing village and resort of Newbiggin-by-the-Sea. This excellent B&B is open all year round. No pets.

The Alnwick Garden
Denwick Lane, Alnwick,
Northumberland, NE66 2NJ
Tel: 01665 511350
website: www.alnwickgarden.com

The vision is to create a beautiful public space accessible to everyone. A garden which is a place of contemplation, a place of fun, a place of inspiration and education.

The Alnwick Garden in Northumberland is one of the most exciting contemporary gardens to be developed in the last century, a magical landscape created from a unique idea.

The Duchess of Northumberland's vision was to create a beautiful public space accessible to everyone: a garden for contemplation, fun, inspiration and education. The Alnwick Garden was officially opened in October 2002 by its patron HRH The Prince of Wales, as the first phase of development was complete. The Garden is now halfway to completion and features spectacular water displays, wonderful gardens and one of the largest tree houses in the world.

The world renowned Belgian designer Jacques Wirtz and his son Peter were chosen to create The Garden, interpreting the Duchess's vision for the 12-acre walled site which was a forgotten and derelict plot before The Alnwick Garden project began work in 2000. Wirtz International's design has transformed it into an exciting scene, dancing with water and ringing with the sounds of life. The Garden is a sequence of busy and quiet spaces, with the gentle and introspective Rose Garden feeling far remote from the children playing in the water jets of the Grand Cascade. An important element of the Wirtz design is the strong green structure which unifies The Garden's diverse themes, visible in the beech hedges, clipped hornbeams and yew. In winter, this structure is evident and visitors are able to see the bones of The Garden, while in summer it provides the backdrop for exuberant flower displays.

Sir Michael Hopkins, recognised as a leading international architect, has designed The Garden's Pavilion and Visitor Centre which opened in 2006. These stunning contemporary buildings house excellent visitor facilities for eating, shopping, learning and relaxing, and places to find out more about other things to do in the region.

However The Garden is more than a garden, and in a relatively short space of time has become recognised not only for gardening excellence but also as a transformational project using its resources to provide real, measurable benefit for people. The vision is being taken forward by The Alnwick Garden Trust who continue to fundraise to complete The Garden by 2009. The Garden is contributing to the regeneration of a rural community as tourism takes on a new level of importance, and as well as being a meeting place for local people provides an opportunity for people of all ages and abilities to experience the arts, enjoy learning new skills and get outdoors for activity or relaxation, and for families to play together.

All surplus revenue is channelled back into the project, helping The Trust go from vision to reality.

83 THE MARKET TAVERN

7 Fenkle Street, Alnwick,
Northumberland NE66 1HW
Tel: 01665 602759 Fax: 0871 5288340
e-mail: enquiries@the-market-tavern.co.uk
website: www.market-tavern.co.uk

The **Market Tavern** has long been known as one of the most popular hostelries in the region, and that reputation has been even more firmly cemented since landlord David Ives and his wife Sue took over the lease in January 2008. Both members of the Association of British Innkeepers, they guarantee a warm welcome for all who pass through the door, whether they be familiar faces or first-timers. There's always plenty of banter between the hosts, the staff and the customers, and Dave, a keen motorcyclist, is always ready to indulge in 'bike talk'. Everyone, young and old, is instantly made to feel at home, and that includes families with children and dogs in the front bar.

Behind the black-and-white frontage the late-18th century inn is surprisingly spacious, with traditional and more contemporary elements combining to pleasant effect. The main bar is on two levels, with steps leading up to a separate dining space, while outside is a small area where smokers can light up. The bar stocks a good selection of real ales, cask beers, lagers and cider, as well as wines, spirits and soft drinks. In the 36-cover restaurant local ingredients are the basis of hearty, value-for-money dishes that are served daily in summer and with prior notice out of season.

The inn stands in the historic centre of Alnwick, close to the Castle (familiar to millions as Hogwarts School in the Harry Potter films), the wonderful Alnwick Garden and the Thursday and Saturday market. Alnwick still retains the look and feel of a great military and commercial centre, and Fenkle Street is typical of the ancient narrow streets in the centre. The town is well worth taking time to explore, and this fine old inn provides a convenient base with its five comfortable, unfussy bedrooms for B&B guests, four of them with en suite facilities.

As well as being a great place for a drink, a summer meal or an overnight stay, the Market Tavern is a social hub of the community, with a regular programme of events: Monday is poker night, hosted by Dave; Tuesday is acoustic night – bring your own instrument or voice, or try your hand on the pub's guitar; Wednesday is quiz night, when all you need to bring is your brain.

The inn accepts the major credit cards.

133

84 THE COACH INN

Lesbury, Alnwick,
Northumberland NE66 3PP
Tel: 01665 830865 Fax: 01665 830866
e-mail: susanpackard@btconnect.com

John and Sue Packard offer a warm welcome and a meal to remember at the **Coach Inn**, which stands in the picturesque village of Lesbury, two miles from the coast and three miles from the centre of Alnwick.

Dating from the middle of the 18th century, when it was a coaching Inn with its own smithy, this delightful free house has immense charm and character, with low beams, original stonework and a snug area with armchairs that's a lovely spot for a quiet drink. First and foremost this is a place to come for a leisurely meal. Food is served from 11 o'clock to last orders at 8.30, and an evening out dining in good company in delightful surroundings is an occasion to savour. One of the signature dishes is slow-roasted Northumbrian lamb, but the menu here is only a guide, and

the chefs are happy to tailor a meal to the personal tastes of their customers using the outstanding locally sourced ingredients that are always available to the kitchen. Booking is recommended at peak times and always for Sunday lunch, which is served from 12 to 5 (in summer to 7). The inn has a wide range of wines and beers (including real ales) to accompany a meal or to enjoy on their own. The bar is open from 11am to 11pm (12 to 10.30 on Sunday). There are seats outside among the pretty flower tubs, and this outstanding inn has ample off-road parking.

86 CEDAR CAFÉ

104 Queen Street, Amble, nr Morpeth,
Northumberland NE65 0DQ
Tel: 01665 710600

Sharon and David Coulson own and run **Cedar Café**, a popular daytime eating place at the bottom of Amble's main street, a short stroll from the harbour, the marina and the beach. Locals and tourists come here to enjoy anything from scones, cakes and toasties to jacket potatoes, Northumbrian steak burger, home-made steak pie, all-day breakfast, the day's roast and always a good choice for vegetarians. Other options include a three-course children's mini-menu and a full Christmas menu served in November and December. Individual items on the menu can be ordered to take away. Cedar Café is open seven days a week, 8.30 to 5.30 (to 4.30 in winter).

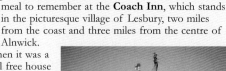

85 THE MASONS ARMS

3 Dial Place, Warkworth, nr Morpeth,
Northumberland NE65 0UR
Tel: 01665 711398
website: www.roxbrohouse.co.uk

The Masons Arms is a distinguished inn at the heart of the historic village of Warkworth. The oldest hostelry in the village, it has a history going back nearly 400 years – it is recorded that the Earl of Derwentwater and 40 of his followers dined here in 1715. The long tradition of hospitality is now in the safe hands of Stuart Metcalfe, who brought many years of catering experience when he took over the lease in 2006. Locals, families, walkers, cyclists, golfers, fishermen and tourists all come here to enjoy the friendly, easygoing ambience and the good choice of food and drink. Real ales and guest beers, lagers, cider, wines by glass and bottle, spirits and soft drinks are served in the bar between 11am and 11pm (to midnight Friday and Saturday and from noon to 11pm on Sunday).

The Masons Arms has a strong following among diners, many of whom travel 20 miles or more to enjoy hearty, value-for-money dishes served every lunchtime and evening. The main menu

proposes pub classics like salmon fishcakes, battered cod, lasagne, chilli con carne, honey-roast ham, steaks and home-made steak pie – a particular favourite. There's always a choice for vegetarians, and traditional desserts include sticky toffee pudding, spotted dick, apple pie and locally made ice cream. Basket meals, jacket potatoes, baguettes and salads provide lighter options.

Warkworth is well worth taking time to explore. There are delightful walks along the banks of the River Coquet and among the sights to be seen are the extensive remains of the Castle, the Church of St Lawrence and The Hermitage, a tiny chapel hewn out of solid rock.

For guests staying overnight, or longer, the Masons Arms has a sister establishment a four-minute walk along the road. **Roxbro House**, a handsome Grade II listed stone building overlooking the Castle, provides superb Bed & Breakfast accommodation in quiet, discreet surroundings, with lots of little extras to guarantee a memorable stay. Furniture and décor are of the highest standard, and the bedrooms feature top-quality bedding, bathrobes, towels and toiletries; all have wide-screen satellite TV with DVD, clock radio and wireless internet connection. Roxbro has a cosy lounge, a garden room where a multi-choice breakfast is served, a beer garden and a sheltered patio. Fresh flowers and chocolates greet arrivals, adding a romantic touch to a stay in this lovely place.

135

87 COQUET ISLAND

Amble, Northumberland NE65 0PE
Tel: 01912 334300
website: www.rspb.org.uk

More than 20,000 pairs of seabirds nest on **Coquet Island** each year. Many travel from as far away as Africa to nest here, some returning to the same nest site they used the previous year. The island, with its unusual square-towered lighthouse, is owned by the Duke of Northumberland and managed by the RSPB as a nature reserve.

Coquet Island has been a place of sanctuary since the time of St. Cuthbert, who landed there in AD 684. The lighthouse was built in 1841, on the ruins of a 15th century monastery. Some of the monastic building has survived and is now protected as a 'Scheduled Ancient Monument' .

Puffins are the most eye-catching of the island's birds. Over 17,000 pairs of puffins nest in burrows across the island, each rearing a single chick. Puffins gather on the water in the evening forming 'rafts', as they preen, rest or dive for sand eels, their main staple food source. One international traveller is the roseate tern, one of the rarest breeding seabirds in the UK. Around 30 - 40 pairs nest on Coquet Island - representing more than 50% of the total UK population.

You can enjoy the spectacle of the birds of Coquet Island by taking one of the boat trips departing from Amble quayside throughout the summer-details are available from the local Tourist Information Centre in Amble, tel: 01665 712313. Also live images are beamed through CCTV to the Tourist Information Centre.

88 THE PACK HORSE INN

Ellingham, Chathill,
Northumberland NE67 5HA
e-mail: graham-e-simpson@hotmail.co.uk
website: www.packhorseinn-ellingham.co.uk

If you enjoy good food at a reasonable price, the **Pack Horse Inn**, set in the quiet village of Ellingham, is the place for you. The delightful early-18th century traditional hostelry serves no bought-in or pre-prepared food. Everything is freshly prepared each day using the best, locally sourced ingredients, so you might find dishes such as Seahouses smoked salmon or Bamburgh bangers on a menu that changes almost daily to ensure that the freshest, most interesting seasonal food is available.

The two qualified chefs Stuart Reid and Tim Holmes are passionate about food and are always willing to vary dishes on the menu to suit a customer's requirements and to take into account individual likes and dislikes or food intolerances – just ask. Meals are served daily from 12 noon until 2pm and again from 6.30pm to 9pm.

In good weather refreshments can be enjoyed on the terrace in the beer garden. If you are planning to stay in this scenic corner of the country, the Pack Horse has five guest bedrooms, all attractively furnished and equipped with TV and hospitality tray. There is also an adjoining self-contained cottage which sleeps four guests in comfort.

89 HOWICK HALL GARDENS AND ARBORETUM

The Estate Office, Howick, Alnwick,
Northumberland NE66 3LB
Tel: 01665 577285
e-mail: estateoffice@howickuk.com
website: www.howickhallgardens.org

The gardens at Howick are peaceful and tranquil and aimed at garden lovers. The BBC Gardeners' World magazine rated it as one of the top 5 coastal gardens in the country, and the Independent Magazine featured it as 'One of the 10 best gardens to visit in spring'.

Howick was the home of the Grey family and the 5th Earl Grey created Silverwood, a woodland garden where rhododendrons and azaleas flourish and where the now famous 60' high Magnolia campbellii has flowered magnificently in early April for over 15 years. Countess Grey had a great interest in spring bulbs and there is now a spectacular display throughout the grounds, beginning with the Snowdrops in mid February. Summer beauty is provided by the formal gardens and terraces in front of Howick Hall, and also the Bog Garden which has been planted with many unusual species.

The arboretum includes about 65 acres of woodland walks. Most of the trees and shrubs are labelled and were grown from seed collected on joint plant hunting expeditions abroad with Kew Gardens. The 'Earl Grey Tea House' is located in the lovely East Quadrant of Howick Hall and serves snacks, light lunches and afternoon teas – Earl Grey of course!

90 CARA HOUSE

44 Castlegate, Berwick-upon-Tweed,
Northumberland TD15 1JT
Tel: 01289 302749
website: www.carahouse.co.uk

Since 2004 Pamela Thompson has been offering Bed & Breakfast accommodation at **Cara House**, which is located through an archway towards the top end of town a short walk from the town centre and the railway station.

Pamela, whose husband David skippers a fishing boat, welcomes guests from near and far into the warm, comfortable surroundings of the 18th century family home, where three excellent en suite bedrooms are available all year round. The rooms are spacious and well-appointed, spotless, warm and cosy, with TV, radio-alarm clock and hot drinks tray; one is a family suite, another has a handsome brass double bed. Guests have the use of a cosy lounge, and the house

has private off-road parking and secure storage for bicycles.

Cara House is a friendly, unpretentious base for exploring historic Berwick-upon-Tweed, the Scottish Borders and North Northumberland. Berwick is one of England's most beguiling towns, with a long and fascinating history. It deserves a leisurely stay to discover all its attractions, and you couldn't find a more pleasant place to start than Cara House.

137

91 BERWICK BARRACKS 🏛

Berwick Barricks & Borough Museum
The Parade, Berwick-upon-Tweed
Northumberland TD15 IDF

Here, you and your family can experience military life first hand. Berwick is one of the outstanding fortified towns of Europe and a visit to our 'Beat of the Drum' Exhibition at these 18th century barracks re-creates the detail and tradition of days in the barrack room. Come into the Gymnasium Gallery – there are art exhibitions in the summer. See the museum dedicated to the King's Own Scottish Borderers – and don't miss the Clock Block, it houses part of the famous Burrell Collection with further lively and imaginative exhibitions.

94 NORHAM CASTLE 🏛

Norham, Berwick-upon-Tweed,
Northumberland TD15 2JY
Tel: 01289 304493
website: www.english-heritage.org.uk

Commanding a vital ford over the River Tweed, Norham was one of the strongest of the border castles, and the most often attacked by the Scots. Besieged at least thirteen times – once for nearly a year by Robert Bruce – it was called 'the most dangerous and adventurous place in the country'. But even its powerful 12th-century keep and massive towered bailey walls could not resist James IV's heavy cannon, and it fell to him in 1513, shortly before his defeat at Flodden. The extensive 16th century rebuilding which followed, adapting the fortress for its own artillery, is still clearly traceable.

92 LINDISFARNE PRIORY 🏛 ⊩

Lindisfarne, Northumberland TD15 2RX
Tel: 01289 389200

Lindisfarne Priory is one of the Holiest Anglo-Saxon sites in England. When you cross the dramatic causeway to Holy Island, you journey into our spiritual heritage. Few places are as beautiful or have such special significance. The corpse of St. Cuthbert was found undecayed in AD698, and this became one of the most sacred shrines in Christendom. For 1300 years it has been a place of pilgrimage and still is today.

Here you can learn about the Monastery's fantastic wealth and walk in the grounds where brutal Viking raiders plundered the priory, forcing Monks to refuge on the mainland. It is advisable to have a tide table with you when you visit Lindisfarne - at high tide the causeway linking Holy Island to the Northumbrian coast is submerged, cutting the Island off.

There is a sculpture on show entitled "Cuthbert of Farne" which was created by local artist Fenwick Lawson. This sculpture depicts a comtemplative Cuthbert reflecting on his religious life and desire for solitude. His interlaced hands echo the stillness and peace he sought. The Museum features are lively and atmospheric and explain what life was like more than a millenium ago. Open daily except Christmas and New Year, the facilities include parking, toilets, gift shop, souvenir guide and exhibition.

138

Bamburgh, Northumberland NE69 7DF
Tel:01668 214515 Fax: 01668 214060
e-mail: bamburghcastle@aol.com
website: www.bamburghcastle.com

Standing on a rocky outcrop overlooking miles of beautiful sandy beach, **Bamburgh Castle** dominates the Northumbrian landscape. The castle became the passion of the 1st Baron Armstrong who, in the 1890's,

began its renovation and refurbishment. This love of Bamburgh was passed down through the family to the late Lord Armstrong, who personally oversaw the completion of his ancestor's dream.

Today Bamburgh Castle is still the home of the Armstrong family, and visitors are able to enjoy what has been described as the finest castle in all England. The public tour includes the magnificent King's Hall, the Cross Hall, reception rooms, the Bakehouse and Victorian Scullery, as well as the Armoury and Dungeon. Throughout, these rooms contain a wide range of fine china, porcelain and glassware, together with paintings, furniture, tapestries, arms and armour.

The Armstrong Museum, occupying the former Laundry Building, is dedicated to the life and work of the first Lord Armstrong. An inventive engineer, shipbuilder and industrialist, he left a great legacy to the modern age and Tyneside in particular.

The castle is open daily from mid March to the end of October, between 11am and 5pm, and teas and light refreshments are available from The Clock Tower.

Tourist Information Centres

ADDERSTONE
Adderstone Services, Adderstone Garage, Belford,
Northumberland NE70 7JU
e-mail: adderstone@hotmail.com
Tel: 01668 213678

AMBLE
Queen Street Car Park, Amble,
Northumberland NE65 0DQ
e-mail: ambletic@alnwick.gov.uk
Tel:01665 712313

BARNARD CASTLE
Woodleigh, Flatts Road, Barnard Castle,
County Durham DL12 8AA
e-mail: tourism@teesdale.gov.uk
Tel: 01833 690909

BELLINGHAM
Fountain Cottage, Main Street, Bellingham,
Near Hexham, Northumberland NE48 2BQ
e-mail: bellinghamtic@btconnect.com
Tel: 01434 220616

BERWICK-UPON-TWEED
106 Marygate, Berwick upon Tweed,
Northumberland TD15 1BN
e-mail: tourism@berwick-upon-tweed.gov.uk
Tel: 01289 330733

BISHOP AUCKLAND
Town Hall, Ground Floor, Market Place, Bishop
Auckland, County Durham DL14 7NP
e-mail: bishopauckland.touristinfo@durham.gov.uk
Tel: 01388 604922

CORBRIDGE
Hill Street, Corbridge, Northumberland NE45 5AA
e-mail: corbridgetic@btconnect.com
Tel: 01434 632815

CRASTER
Craster Car Park, Craster, Alnwick,
Northumberland NE66 3TW
e-mail: crastertic@alnwick.gov.uk
Tel: 01665 576007

DARLINGTON
Address:The Dolphin Centre, Horsemarket,
Darlington DL1 5RP
e-mail: tic@darlington.gov.uk
Tel: 01325 388666

DURHAM
2 Millennium Place, Durham City DH1 1WA
e-mail: touristinfo@durhamcity.gov.uk
Tel: 0191 384 3720

GATESHEAD
Central Library, Prince Consort Road, Gateshead,
Tyne & Wear NE8 4LN
e-mail: tic@gateshead.gov.uk
Tel: 0191 433 8420

GUISBOROUGH
Priory Grounds, Church Street, Guisborough TS14 6HG
e-mail: guisborough_tic@redcar-cleveland.gov.uk
Tel: 01287 633801

HALTWHISTLE
Railway Station, Station Road, Haltwhistle,
Northumberland NE49 9HN
e-mail: haltwhistletic@btconnect.com
Tel: 01434 322002

HARTLEPOOL
Hartlepool Art Gallery, Church Square,
Hartlepool TS24 7EQ
e-mail: hpooltic@hartlepool.gov.uk
Tel: 01429 869706

HEXHAM
Wentworth Car Park, Hexham
Northumberland NE46 1QE
e-mail: hexham.tic@tynedale.gov.uk
Tel: 01434 652220

MIDDLESBROUGH
(PO Box 69), Middlesbrough Info. Centre & Box Office,
Albert Road, Middlesbrough TS1 2QQ
e-mail: addresstic@middlesbrough.gov.uk
Tel: 01642 729700

MIDDLETON-IN-TEESDALE

10 Market Place, Middleton-in-Teesdale,
County Durham DL12 0QG
e-mail: middletonplus@compuserve.com
Tel: 01833 641001

MORPETH

The Chantry, Bridge Street, Morpeth,
Northumberland NE61 1PD
e-mail: tourism@castlemorpeth.gov.uk
Tel: 01670 500700

NEWCASTLE AIRPORT

Tourist Information Desk, Newcastle Airport,
Newcastle upon Tyne, Tyne & Wear NE13 8BZ
e-mail: niatic@hotmail.com
Tel: 0191 214 4422

NEWCASTLE-UPON-TYNE

Newcastle Information Centre, 8-9 Central Arcade,
Newcastle upon Tyne, Tyne & Wear NE1 5AF
e-mail: tourist.info@newcastle.gov.uk
Tel: 0191 277 8000

NORTH SHIELDS

Unit 18, Royal Quays Outlet Shopping, North Shields,
Tyne & Wear NE29 6DW
e-mail: ticns@northtyneside.gov.uk
Tel: 0191 2005895

ONCE BREWED

Address:Northumberland National Park Centre,
Military Road, Bardon Mill, Hexham,
Northumberland NE47 7AN
e-mail: tic.oncebrewed@nnpa.org.uk
Tel: 01434 344396

OTTERBURN

Otterburn Mill, Otterburn, Northumberland NE19 1JT
e-mail:tic@otterburnmill.co.uk
Tel: 01830 520093

PETERLEE

4 Upper Yoden Way, Peterlee, County Durham SR8 1AX
e-mail: touristinfo@peterlee.gov.uk
Tel: 0191 586 4450

REDCAR

West Terrace, Esplanade, Redcar, Cleveland TS10 3AE
e-mail: redcar_tic@redcar-cleveland.gov.uk
Tel: 01642 471921

ROTHBURY

Northumberland National Park Centre, Church House,
Church Street, Rothbury, Northumberland NE65 7UP
e-mail: tic.rothbury@nnpa.org.uk
Tel: 01669 620887

SALTBURN-BY-SEA

3 Station Buildings, Station Square, Saltburn-by-Sea,
Cleveland TS12 1AQ
e-mail: saltburn_tic@redcar-cleveland.gov.uk
Tel: 01287 622422

SEAHOUSES

Seafield Car Park, Seafield Road, Seahouses,
Northumberland NE68 7SW
e-mail: seahousesTIC@berwick-upon-tweed.gov.uk
Tel: 01665 720884

SOUTH SHIELDS

South Shields Museum & Gallery, Ocean Road,
South Shields, Tyne & Wear NE33 2HZ
e-mail: museum.tic@s-tyneside-mbc.gov.uk
Tel: 0191 454 6612

SOUTH SHIELDS (AMPHITHEATRE)

Sea Road, South Shields, Tyne & Wear NE33 2LD
e-mail: foreshore.tic@s-tyneside-mbc.gov.uk
Tel: 0191 455 7411

STANHOPE

Durham Dales Centre, Castle Gardens, Stanhope,
County Durham DL13 2FJ
e-mail: durham.dales.centre@durham.gov.uk
Tel: 01388 527650

STOCKTON-ON-TEES

Stockton Central Library, Church Road,
Stockton-on-Tees TS18 1TU
e-mail: touristinformation@stockton.gov.uk
Tel: 01642 528130

SUNDERLAND

50 Fawcett Street, Sunderland, Tyne & Wear SR1 1RF
e-mail: tourist.info@sunderland.gov.uk
Tel: 0191 553 2000

WHITLEY BAY

Park Road, Whitley Bay, Tyne & Wear NE26 1EJ
e-mail: ticwb@northtyneside.gov.uk
Tel: 0191 2008535

WOOLER

Wooler TIC, The Cheviot Centre, 12 Padgepool Place,
Wooler, Northumberland NE71 6BL
e-mail: woolerTIC@berwick-upon-tweed.gov.uk
Tel: 01668 282123

Towns, Villages and Places of Interest

TRAVEL PUBLISHING ORDER FORM

To order any of our publications just fill in the payment details below and complete the order form. For orders of less than 4 copies please add £1.00 per book for postage and packing. Orders over 4 copies are P & P free.

Name:

Address:

Tel no:

Please Complete Either:

I enclose a cheque for £ _____ made payable to Travel Publishing Ltd

Or:

Card No: Expiry Date:

Signature:

Please either send, telephone, fax or e-mail your order to:

Travel Publishing Ltd, Airport Business Centre, 10 Thornbury Road, Estover, Plymouth PL6 7PP

Tel: 01752 697280   Fax: 01752 697299   e-mail: info@travelpublishing.co.uk

	Price	Quantity		Price	Quantity
HIDDEN PLACES REGIONAL TITLES			**COUNTRY LIVING RURAL GUIDES**		
Cornwall	£8.99	....	East Anglia	£10.99	....
Devon	£8.99	....	Heart of England	£10.99	....
Dorset, Hants & Isle of Wight	£8.99	....	Ireland	£11.99	....
East Anglia	£8.99	....	North East	£10.99	....
Lake District & Cumbria	£8.99	....	North West	£10.99	....
Northumberland & Durham	£8.99	....	Scotland	£11.99	....
Peak District and Derbyshire	£8.99	....	South of England	£10.99	....
Yorkshire	£8.99	....	South East of England	£10.99	....
HIDDEN PLACES NATIONAL TITLES			Wales	£11.99	....
England	£11.99	....	West Country	£10.99	....
Ireland	£11.99	....			
Scotland	£11.99	....			
Wales	£11.99	....	**TOTAL QUANTITY:**		
OTHER TITLES			**POST & PACKING:**		
Off the Motorway	£11.99	....	**TOTAL VALUE:**		
Garden Centres & Nurseries	£11.99	....			

VISIT THE TRAVEL PUBLISHING WEBSITE

Looking for:

- *Places to Visit?*
- *Places to Stay?*
- *Places to Eat & Drink?*
- *Places to Shop?*

Then why not visit the Travel Publishing website...

- Informative pages on places to visit, stay, eat, drink and shop throughout the British Isles.

- Detailed information on Travel Publishing's wide range of national and regional travel guides.

www.travelpublishing.co.uk

HIDDEN PLACES GUIDES

Explore Britain and Ireland with *Hidden Places* guides - a fascinating series of national and local travel guides.

Packed with easy to read information on hundreds of places of interest as well as places to stay, eat and drink.

Available from both high street and internet booksellers

For more information on the full range of *Hidden Places* guides and other titles published by Travel Publishing visit our website on

www.travelpublishing.co.uk
or ask for our leaflet by phoning **01752 276660** or emailing **info@travelpublishing.co.uk**

READER REACTION FORM

The *Travel Publishing* research team would like to receive reader's comments on any visitor attractions or places reviewed in the book and also recommendations for suitable entries to be included in the next edition. This will help ensure that the *Country Living series of Guides* continues to provide its readers with useful information on the more interesting, unusual or unique features of each attraction or place ensuring that their visit to the local area is an enjoyable and stimulating experience. To provide your comments or recommendations would you please complete the forms below and overleaf as indicated and send to:

The Research Department, Travel Publishing Ltd,
Airport Business Centre, 10 Thornbury Road, Estover, Plymouth PL6 7PP

Your Name:

Your Address:

Your Telephone Number:

Please tick as appropriate:

Comments ☐   Recommendation ☐

Name of Establishment:

Address:

Telephone Number:

Name of Contact:

READER REACTION FORM

COMMENT OR REASON FOR RECOMMENDATION:

....
....
....
....
....
....
....
....
....
....
....
....
....
....
....
....
....
....
....

READER REACTION FORM

The *Travel Publishing* research team would like to receive reader's comments on any visitor attractions or places reviewed in the book and also recommendations for suitable entries to be included in the next edition. This will help ensure that the *Country Living series of Guides* continues to provide its readers with useful information on the more interesting, unusual or unique features of each attraction or place ensuring that their visit to the local area is an enjoyable and stimulating experience. To provide your comments or recommendations would you please complete the forms below and overleaf as indicated and send to:

The Research Department, Travel Publishing Ltd,
Airport Business Centre, 10 Thornbury Road, Estover, Plymouth   PL6 7PP

Your Name:

Your Address:

Your Telephone Number:

Please tick as appropriate:

Comments ☐   Recommendation ☐

Name of Establishment:

Address:

Telephone Number:

Name of Contact:

READER REACTION FORM

COMMENT OR REASON FOR RECOMMENDATION:

....

....

....

....

....

....

....

....

....

....

....

....

....

....

....

....

READER REACTION FORM

The *Travel Publishing* research team would like to receive reader's comments on any visitor attractions or places reviewed in the book and also recommendations for suitable entries to be included in the next edition. This will help ensure that the *Country Living series of Guides* continues to provide its readers with useful information on the more interesting, unusual or unique features of each attraction or place ensuring that their visit to the local area is an enjoyable and stimulating experience. To provide your comments or recommendations would you please complete the forms below and overleaf as indicated and send to:

The Research Department, Travel Publishing Ltd,
Airport Business Centre, 10 Thornbury Road, Estover, Plymouth PL6 7PP

Your Name:

Your Address:

Your Telephone Number:

Please tick as appropriate:

Comments ☐   Recommendation ☐

Name of Establishment:

Address:

Telephone Number:

Name of Contact:

READER REACTION FORM

COMMENT OR REASON FOR RECOMMENDATION:

....

....

....

....

....

....

....

....

....

....

....

....

....

....

....

....

....

....

READER REACTION FORM

The *Travel Publishing* research team would like to receive reader's comments on any visitor attractions or places reviewed in the book and also recommendations for suitable entries to be included in the next edition. This will help ensure that the *Country Living series of Guides* continues to provide its readers with useful information on the more interesting, unusual or unique features of each attraction or place ensuring that their visit to the local area is an enjoyable and stimulating experience. To provide your comments or recommendations would you please complete the forms below and overleaf as indicated and send to:

**The Research Department, Travel Publishing Ltd,
Airport Business Centre, 10 Thornbury Road, Estover, Plymouth PL6 7PP**

Your Name:

Your Address:

Your Telephone Number:

Please tick as appropriate:

Comments ☐   Recommendation ☐

Name of Establishment:

Address:

Telephone Number:

Name of Contact:

READER REACTION FORM

COMMENT OR REASON FOR RECOMMENDATION:

....
....
....
....
....
....
....
....
....
....
....
....
....
....
....
....
....
....

Index of Advertisers

PLACES OF INTEREST